A VIEW FROM

THE RIDGE

By the same authors:

Mountain Days and Bothy Nights (1987)

Irene

This book is dedicated, with love, to Peter Angus and Oonagh – and once again to all pictured within its covers who gave us the benefit of their experience.

A

VIEW FROM

THE RIDGE

Dave Brown & Ian Mitchell

Illustrations by Maggie Ramage

THE ERNEST PRESS

Published by The Ernest Press 1991

British Library Cataloguing in Publication Data

Brown, Dave
  The view from the ridge.
  I. Mitchell, Ian Robert
  796.522

  ISBN 0 94815 311 3

Typeset by EMS Phototypesetting, Berwick upon Tweed.
Printed by Martin's of Berwick Ltd.
Bound by Hunter & Foulis, Edinburgh.

Contents

Acknowledgements

We would like to express our deepest thanks to Clare MacLean and Pat Heppell, who subjected the manuscript to a literary criticism that was both searching and beneficial. The responsibility for any residual sexism or pure bad taste is entirely our own.

We would also like to thank Erchie Boomer for help with tales of the Auld Crowd, and for being Erchie.

Last we thank Faber and Faber for permission to quote from *The Collected Poems* of T.S. Eliot.

Preface: Out of Eden

Most mountaineering literature falls into one of three categories: the epic, the metaphysical or the couthy. One might see Messner, Murray and MacGregor as their three respective muses. But whatever the category, there usually lies behind mountain literature – and outdoor literature in general – a fundamental shared philosophy, different though its modes of expression may be. This philosophy is that the experience of mountaineering (or of Nature) releases the participant from the pressures and tensions of life in general, and of urban life in particular.

We live in a peculiar culture in Britain. Since the late eighteenth century the countryside has been portrayed as a rural Eden largely free of the tensions, ugliness and conflicts of urban life, ('Hell is a city'). This has led to an over-valuation of the rural, as against an undervaluation of urban, experience.

Both the writers of the present work value and are, we hope, sensitive to the landscape and culture of rural, and especially mountain, life. But we do not think Hell is a city, nor that the transfer of urban culture in any form to rural life is a blot on Arcadia. Moreover, and in this we hope our present work can claim a small measure of uniqueness, we both fundamentally dismiss the idea that, knapsack on your back, you leave all troubles and social ills behind when you head for the mountains. When on the hills you take with you the baggage of problems and tensions that drive you to seek their solace. And you find, not a rural Utopia, but another set of social relations with their own problems, conflicts, ugliness – and strengths.

Nature is thus, for us, not an escape from, but a reflection of, wider social issues and concerns. This view is what, we hope, gives an underlying unifying tension to the divergent chapters of the book. These chapters describe, not a shared experience, but an overlapp-

1

ing residue of sentiment. While we might not agree with everything the other says, we are in solidarity with the respective attempts made to say it. We hope the readers will respect the integrity of the endeavour we have made to give our View from the Ridge, and find something in it to echo their own experience. If you look for Eden, you will be disappointed. But if you know what you can – and cannot – find, you might achieve a modest victory.

Mair o' The Same? A Dialogue

The Scene: A mountain hut in Scotland. A fire. Two men. Two glasses. Silence. (One man rearranges the wood on the fire).

First man: Birk and Rodden. Nae use unless ye've got pine as weel, they jist smoulder. (Pause). Ah weel, it's us twa again.

Second man: Aye, and I thought they'd be fighting tae get awa wi us, noo that we're famous. I wouldnae hae thought yon book we wrote would dae sae weel.

First man: Third in the best-seller lists: fa would o' thocht it? And maist folk said they liked it. "Gie us mair!", some cried.

Second man: Mind you, I was a bit worried that the Creag Dhu called it 'Spycatcher', for revealing their secrets. I thought they might send a hit man.

First man: But onybody likes tae be famous. Immortality we've gien them a', a priceless thing.

Second man: Famous is wan thing, but infamous is anither. Maybe they're feart tae come noo, in case we write aboot them. 'A chiel's amang you takkin notes, an' faith he'll prent it,' as Burns said.

First man: But it did lead tae some reunions and renewed contact; even folk like Mealy Pudding and the Big Yin took it in good spirits. That's something we could write aboot, if we ever dae anither book; reunions, fit happened tae auld pals.

Second man: The critics certainly liked the first ane. (Quoting) 'Unneutered political Scots', 'Many fine tales are told', 'Always entertaining, if not laudable activities...',

First man: I was a bit disappyntet in the critics; the comedy was
               a' they took heed o'. They missed the fact that the
               book was the Great Scottish Novel in disguise, the
               uncreated consciousness of the race, in the Joycean
               sense. Then the Gramscian aspect was o'erlooked,
               the struggle for the cultural hegemony of the proleta-
               riat in an area of bourgeois society.

Second man: Weel, ye'd expect them tae miss a' that. But the style,
               the mock-heroic parody o' the knightly search for the
               Holy Grail, ye would think they'd o' grasped that. If
               we dae write something else, we'll hae tae be mair
               obviously weighty, or the critics will jist regard us as
               comic writers. You could dae something aboot yer
               wee boy. Takkin him oot and passing things on. Nae
               jokes, and some meditations on man and nature as
               weel. Tae show that we're no jist narrow eccentrics
               but all-round renaissance eccentrics.

First man: Time tae licht a caundle.
               (He gets up to do so, and at the same time replenishes
               the glasses.)

First man: We need new angles, but we could still dae something
               mair on bothies and the auld days. And the Great
               Sutherland Transport and Trading Company Bike-
               Tube Saga must be told! But we need tae avoid a
               repeat o' the first book, simply mair o' the same. That
               nivver works.
               (Silence falls again.)

Second man: Something else was disappointing. I thought that the
               lovelies threw themselves on ye if ye were a famous
               author. Mind you, the picture on the front didnae
               exactly capture oor craggy good looks, did it?

First man: The weemen were quite critical despite us showing
               the tender side of post-macho man. They said there
               were nae weemen in it; ane said it was 'A celebration

of male culture'.

Second man: (Interrupting) There was a wumman in it, the wan wi the dug!

First man: I tried tae be sympathetic, and suggested that they burn their bras at the bookshops. But they said I was jist aifter the publicity. Basic trust is lacking atween the sexes...

Second man: But they need their bras noo: they cannae defy gravity when they're past 30. Nae mair bra burning, its the Janet Raeger catalogues noo.

First man: Aye. (Pause) Great, intit?

Second man: Aye. But seriously though, and let's try and be serious, cut doon the funny stuff, that'd be a good angle. Wummen and their attitudes tae the hills, 'Sex and the Single Bothy Girl'.

First man: If you deal wi the sex, I'll dae the meditations on man and nature. We should each dae fit we're good at. (Further adjustment of the fire takes place. Another silence.)

Second man: I met wan o' the Auld Crowd, and he liked the book. I was at the funeral o' wan o' them recently. I'd like tae write that up, and the hale story o' that team. They are remarkable men.

First man: And then there's the young team, tae balance that, something aboot the generation gap, and young lads realising there's mair tae life than stretchy pants and chalk, under the guidance o' mature men. Ane wi melow features, wi hidden depths, like a Cairngorm hill...

Second man: The ither wi bold rugged features, like a West Coast crag. Robert Redford and Clint Eastwood would be great for the film o' the book.

First man: Are they nae a bit auld noo?

(A lengthy pause)

Fit aboot some tea?

(He goes to the table and busies himself there).

Second man: (Musing) And then there's how it a' started. Very first experiences...And fa'in aff, accidents...And then fights, there used tae be some great fights...We could ca it 'Fighting, Falling and Fucking!'

First man: Keep it clean and keep it serious! And we've got tae widen the market. I think something aboot using bikes and trains tae get intae the hills, and even boats, showing that ye can dae athoot the car. That would appeal tae cyclists, sailors and train lovers.

I think we've got something, something mair varied than the first ane, broader and maybe deeper. We'll ca it 'A View From the Ridge'. It'll be a meditation on the mountains in mid-life, a miscellany...Showing hoo there's nae rural Arcadia and hoo mountain life jist reproduces the contradictions o' the wider society...

Second man: Nivver mind the mountain miscellany, whar's the mountain dew?

(He picks up and shoogles the bottle)

Finished! A good drap o' the malt that, nane o' yer White Man's Firewater. Wi the price o' a good dram, and the Janet Raeger, we'll need tae keep writing. Aye, we'll gie it a try. But I'll tell ye wan thing. It'll no win the Tasker-Boardman Memorial Prize.

(The light fades).

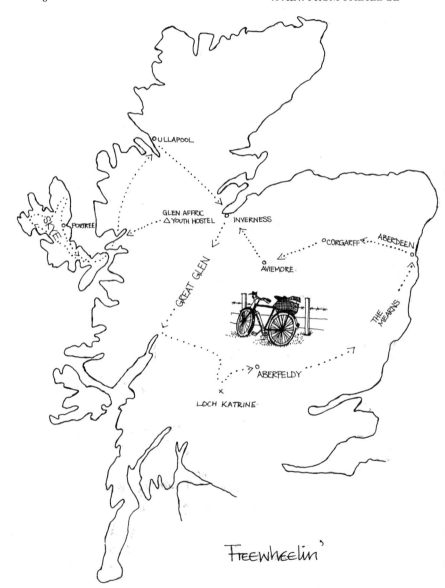

Freewheelin'

Freewheelin

'Where have you been, my blue-eyed son?....
I've stumbled on the side of twelve misty mountains.'
(Dylan *A Hard Rain*)

What can I remember about that summer nearly thirty years ago? I used to have a map with the route marked on it but lost that and can not remember exactly where we went. But maybe if I think hard some of it will come back, some of the route, the incidents of that trip where it all started – or rather, where the seeds were laid....

We, that is the two of us, were Dan and I and we were fifteen. We got to know each other as bursary boys, the old birds of a feather rule. We flocked together against the public school and its pupils with whom we fell into an equilibrium of mutual disfavour. Well here we were, without the hated uniform and discipline and alien tongue forced into our heads, off free-wheeling in the summer holidays. A whole month of it away from school and away from parents as well, on our bikes into the wild Highlands where we were convinced we would find adventure and sentimental education. Mentally we thought we were mature, prepared like Quentin in *Absalom, Absalom!*, who said he was older than most people who had died. Faulkner could have been describing us, we thought.

Well-equipped we were not. I had a Raleigh Sports bike, of colossal weight, of the kind often derogatorily referred to as a 'minister's bike' (for in those days ministers still often travelled by bike, as did insurance salesmen). Dan was better equipped; he had a racing bike, the accidentally limited edition Blue Streak, withdrawn when Britain's independent nuclear deterrent failed to perform in the Australian desert. The symbolism of this escaped us at the time; but, like the Profumo scandal, it was a harbinger of the end of an era. The Tories, in power all our cogniscent lives, were about to fall and the 60s to begin.

That apart, we had a cheese-cloth tent without flysheet or groundsheet – but more of that later. We had no stove, thinking to cook by fires like those hobos in the novels by Steinbeck and Hemingway we were devouring. Round the fire we would have conversations about the great works we would soon write, about existentialism (Dan had just acquired *Six Existentialist Thinkers*) and anarchism (I imagined myself Bakunin's last follower at that time.) And about sex; about how we might contrive not to remain virgins all our lives. With a few pounds (I think I had twelve) and SYHA cards for emergencies, we set off on the high road to Strathdon one July morning; the high road of expectation.

It may seem foolhardy to have undertaken such an adventure at such a tender age, but remember that then there was still little traffic, at least in the Highlands. Even in Aberdeen we could still play football with lamp-posts as goals, stopping only for the buses to pass. Most traders still came round with horse-drawn carts on the scheme where I lived and my father, with a works van, was the first in the street to have access to four wheels. There were lorries, albeit no juggernauts, and most of the traffic we passed on our journey consisted of the odd bus, tractors, mobile shops and an occasional commercial traveller.

I know we started up Donside for the Cock Bridge to Tomintoul road, to camp at Corgarff the first night, 55 miles away. I remember nothing of that journey except a stop at the Brig o' Alford, where Murray's couthy poems were written – poems of happy herd laddies in a mythical rural Arcadia. Poems for which we had nothing but contempt though they were offered us at school as the acceptable face of Doric. Our speech was slang and use of it a beltable offence. Once a German linguist came to our school, and told us that our patois was older than standard English, which was derived from it and that we should speak it. When he'd gone, the English master said, 'Forget what he said, boys.' We got lost at Muir of Fowlis, till a local told us, "Ye're gyan the wrang gait. It's hyn doon t'ither road."

Corgarff seemed like the American outback. No cars, stooks in the fields, horses still working the land. And the shop where we sought our meal, selling nothing but imperishable tins. Nothing fresh or frozen. Except the face of the shopkeeper when we asked for beer and she refused to sell it to us. We spent the evening picking twigs and burnt wood out of our soup. But were too tired to have a discussion on existentialism, and went to bed early.

Next we went over the Lecht to Tomintoul, seeing not a vehicle on the way, but hundreds of blue hares which Dan thought we should pursue with sharpened sticks; he had fantasies of living off the land, like Tom Sawyer and Huck Finn. To this end we had taken a hand line with us. With it we later caught a couple of shitey sadies at Ullapool, but they smelled so bad when we cooked them that we threw them away.

We reached Aviemore that night, a sleepy underdeveloped town, and camped in a wood outside amidst neatly piled heaps of pine needles. Dan awoke first, complaining, "Something's chawing my cock!"

(He had the adolescent male's neurosis about threats to his unused member.)

His must have been tastier than mine, because at first I did not feel anything. But on rousing into sleep-sodden awakening, I noticed that the tent was black with ants, obviously furious at our intrusion into their domain. We fled the tent in our underpants, brushing the ants off. I remember it was a beautiful morning; or rather night, for it was about four o'clock. The first time I had seen a dawn.

Repeated forays retrieved our clothes, equipment and dismantled the tent. We carried thousands of ants with us to our next camping-spot burning them to death with candles in a holocaust that evening. We tried the same tactic with the midgies one night in Skye when they were very bad but gave up and spent the night in a telephone box nearby. These candle-chamber massacres reduced even further the dubious waterproofing of our tent.

Little remains in memory of the next stage, to Inverness. We stayed at the Hostel, hoping that it would be full of young girls as sex-obsessed as we were. But only Frauleins asking, "And what is the winter like in your country?" or mesdemoiselles saying, "And how many francs do you get for a pound?" inhabited the sex-free establishment. I doubt if sex has ever taken place within the walls of a Youth Hostel, which is probably why so many unescorted girls are allowed to frequent them. We also had the indignity there of being refused entry to a pub, when we were already regulars of the Well of Spa Bar in Aberdeen, sharing the howff with carters and coalmen, and musicians from His Majesty's Theatre at interval time. And we frequented the low harbour dives, discussing Jean-Paul Sartre, or Fidel Castro and Che Guevara, heroes after events in Cuba, wondering why the tarts did not take us seriously as potential customers or the trawlermen want to converse about the iniquities of capitalist exploitation.

The weather had been kind but then the rain started and the wind. We battled up Glen Cannich drookit and frozen and, rounding a bend, my panniers fell off scattering their contents over the road. We were repairing the damage when a man approached. We had been seen from his window and he took us in to dry off by a fire, gave us tea and scones. He chatted to us but we could not understand a word, or hardly, since a bullet had gone through his tongue in the war. That much we managed to get. The war to us was more than a lifetime away though both our fathers took part. He gave us some Buddy Holly and Elvis records to play while we waited for the weather to clear. I was getting too sophisticated for this. I'd already heard a Bob Dylan L.P., *Freewheelin*, which had overwhelmed me. After the Cuba Crisis, when we all thought we were going to die and our maths teacher had sat with head in hands and had cancelled lessons, *A Hard Rain* had bowled me over. Here was what it was all about, someone else understood, thought like me. Dan was more a Stones man; they appealed to his attempt to affect amoral hedonism.

We carried on, pulling up the hard road to Cannich and up past the hydro dams till we came to the eastern end of Loch Affric, some miles after where the road then ended. But we were intending to rough bike it, cross to Kintail by the old drove road past Alltbeithe, and thence on to Skye. Real wild rovers, we were! We had passed no one all afternoon, bar an American singing as he ascended the Glen. At the lodge we met the post-office van, and asked the occupant the way. "There's no road beyond here," he assured us. We mentioned that we wanted to go to Skye and he looked horrified, "But there's only the road to Kintail!" he muttered, as if talking of the road to hell. "You'll never get through on bikes!"

We assured him we would and he sadly directed us to the old path (at that time there was no forestry track to the south of the loch) on the north side of the loch. And off we went. Here we were, just like the Oakies, just like Nick Adams. This was real life, not that second-rate public school we had been misfortunate to have been bright enough to get to and where our parents had elected to send us. We were the truants, the miscreants, but since we did not play by the rules, we got off with it. Dan once came late for an exam, claiming he'd had a puncture. He was to be belted till he produced the bike with the flat tyre. (He had the sense to stick his protractor through it outside the school gates.)

We pushed the bikes along the lochside, mounting every now and again where traces of the old pony-and-trap track still remained. I remember looking at the mountains, impossibly high, and wondering if I would ever aspire to gaining the summits. Their names were unknown to me but the sight of them awoke wonder. But the road demanded more attention. Carrying the bikes, with panniers, on our shoulders through the bog the last mile or so to the youth hostel, we fell frequently; Dan less so since his bike was lighter. We got there. Everyone who arrived after brought something fallen from our bikes; food, a shoe, a book.

The warden was an old man, at least as old as our parents (in retrospect, probably mid-forties); a Glaswegian who told us he hadn't seen anyone for two weeks. In the height of summer! He walked to the loch then took a boat to the lodge for his supplies and dreamed of having a donkey for the journey one day. He was pleased to see us, and the others who arrived, including the singing American who went off to fish. I can not recall everyone there. Maybe there were a dozen, including two women, older mature ones in their twenties. Our hopes rose. We had heard many tales about older women, past their prime, and their desire to initiate young men into the mysteries of sexual experience.

That night started like our wildest dreams realised. The American came in with fish which were gutted and fried, then eaten all round. A fire was lit and the warden and a couple of older men told tales of mountain ascents, wild bivouacs and epic cross-country expeditions. The warden produced a bottle of whisky and handed it round. That in the bottom of our mugs remained untasted though raised to lips. We thought only McEwan's Export worthy of our palates.

We cast longing glances at the women but somehow could not compete for social space with the exotic foreigners and wild mountain men. We became aware of the paucity of our experience. When we went to bed, long after midnight, we were enlivened and chastened at the same time. "Aye," said Dan sadly, "We'll jist hae tae keep yarkin oor puddins." I was thinking that maybe if we could climb a few of those mountains we had seen then we could impress the opposite sex with our manliness....

Again, I do not remember much of the next day, except that it was hell. Pushing our bikes at the good bits, carrying them through bogs and across rivers at the worst bits. We were lucky the weather was good, especially as we had no map bar a thirty miles to the inch SYHA Scotland one which showed a glen after Glen Affric slanting south-west to Kintail. We took it and reached Kintail knackered. But we had to carry on to Kyle. Next day would be Sunday and on the Sabbath there was no ferry to the Misty Isle. We got there late and boarded the wee boat that took four cars or one bus and left the mainland for the first time in our lives. Even Dan was excited, despite his world-weary cynicism bred on Henry Miller.

I have been back dozens of times but the impact of that time still lingers. Not details, precious few of them I remember, but the impression. The roads, grass-grown on the crown and potholed; one after Broadford knocked me off my bike. The still, to us, ubiquitous Gaelic. Everyone seemed to speak it but drop into English when we arrived. The grey must on the green and brown moors, sloping to the grey sea. Dunvegan we made but baulked at the entry fee to the castle; round Trotternish we pedalled, marvelling at Storr and wondering if anyone else had noticed it. Everywhere the pyramids in the fields were hay stooks and not yet tents.

We decided to hire a boat, row out to Prince Charlie's cave, to fish. So down to the harbour we went. We had experience on the Duthie Park pond so we knew we could handle Portree Bay. At the pier it said. BOATS FOR HIRE; so far so good. And a man stood by, by dress and mien identifiable as a local. Obviously the owner of the boats. Dan approached him, "Are these boats for hire?"

"Oh yes, they'll be for hire."

"How much?"

"Oh well, I wouldn't be knowing that now."

Dan was bewildered, wondering if bargaining was expected. "But what do you normally charge?" – exasperatedly.

"Oh well I don't charge, they're not my boats."

"Do you know whose they are?"

"Oh yes. I'll be knowing that."

"Well, who owns the boats then?" Dan was an impatient youth.

"It'll be Hamish who owns the boats."

"Where is he? When will he be back?"

"Oh I'll not be sure when he'll be back. Sometime."

"Do you think we could take a boat and then pay Hamish when we come back?"

"Oh no. Hamish wouldn't be liking that at all at all."

So we gave up at our first encounter with teuchter impenetrability and fished off the pier.

From Strome to Ullapool little remains in memory except a puncture at Braemore. Not a big deal you might say, but we had no puncture outfits and I pushed the bike to Ullapool – about ten miles. Naturally, there was no shop in Ullapool that sold cycle tubes. We had a choice. I could get the bus to Inverness and back and buy one. But that was ruled out as extravagantly costly. Or the local shop would take an order, which would arrive in three days. We pitched our tent on a hillside outside Ullapool and waited.

It started to rain. Ark-building rain, rain like we had never seen. Solid rain, leaving hardly space for air. We felt as if we were underwater. We spent the first day in the tent digging drainage channels for the water to flow out. We covered the tent with our tippets and ourselves with plastic bags to try and keep dry; to no avail. It relented a little in the night and we slept a soggy sleep but next day it was again a monsoon.

We had not been able to cook for twenty-four hours, eating only biscuits and bread. But now nature was calling in its various ways, forcing us to go outside. And Dan had a brilliant idea. Crouching in a primitive posture and utilising an empty cornflake packet, he managed to deposit his rectal debris in the receptacle and chuck it outside into the lashing rain. Fine pleased, he retreated to his damp sleeping bag. I had a different problem; a liquid one, but decided to follow his example. I picked up an empty strawberry tin, bent the jagged edge back, and kneeling at the door began to pee into it, to great relief. It began to fill rapidly; more rapidly than I was emptying, and I lurched forward trying to control my bladder and avoid the jagged lid contacting my private parts. I was soon lying in a puddle of piss outside with the rain lashing down. Dan looked up with amusement from his *Men Without Women*.

This could not go on. We were squalid, sodden, hungry. So we abandoned the tent and its contents, YH cards in our pockets, and headed for Ullapool. Firstly the chip shop was visited and sustenance gained. Then we headed, defeated, for the hostel itself. And that was where it happened. Sex reared its, to us, lovely head. There were women there and we managed to engage a couple of them in conversation. Dan's one I didn't fancy, but mine was just like Christine Keeler. They were greatly impressed by our manly feats of physical endurance and we had thoughts of luring them back to our tent when the monsoon passed. I went upstairs to get the map and show them our impressive route, and in my haste to return tumbled hielstergowdie downstairs.

The leg was not painful at first; just niggly. But it got worse in the next couple of weeks and when I got home, 500 miles later, I could hardly stand on it. I had sustained a multiple fracture of the hip; it would be two years before I cycled again.

The women? They showed no interest in coming to see our soggy tent. When the tube came we struck camp and headed again for Inverness.

"Maybe if we wash we'll hae mair luck?" I suggested.

"Na," came back Dan, "it's manly smells that gets them roused."

I deferred to his judgement, based on his reading of Henry Miller.

Thence we headed on our homeward leg, down the Great Glen. On that homeward stretch certain incidents stand out in the memory. At Killin we faced a crisis.

Money was getting short due to the extravagances of hostel nights; we were facing starvation, out of contact with home. I recalled having been with my parents to Loch Katrine and noticing that where the 'Walter Scott' was berthed the loch floor was covered in money. Dan fell in with my plan and we made a fifty-mile detour to the loch, where we camped hidden in the woods and waited for night to fall.

Fall it did and the tourists departed. We hid in the bushes till the lights in the café and supervisor's house went out. Then we crawled forward close to the ground, torches in hand, till we reached the water. Off came our clothes and in we went. One thing our school had taught us was to swim and the life-saving training came in handy, diving to the bottom and surfacing with handfuls of dirt, stones and coins. Again and again we dived, despite the cold, until we could take it no more. Donning our clothes we pocketed our ill-gotten gains and headed back for the tent, rising early in the morning to avoid imagined pursuit. We had gained over five pounds; enough to last us till home. For the rest of the trip purchases were paid for in rusty pennies and ha'pennies.

"Meat," said Dan one day. "We need meat, fresh meat. We'll get scurvy if we dinnae hae some fresh meat."

Dan's obsessions always had a psuedo-scientific basis. Now I was as fed up as he of tinned meatballs heated over a fire, but the mysteries of cooking were unknown to us. It seemed very adventurous. But there we stood, serried piles of coins on the butcher's counter, before departing with our stewing steak and potatoes for the tent.

Commandos

"Ye just pit the lot in and bile it up thegither," announced Dan once the fire was going. I waited on the boil and threw in the non-too-clean potatoes. While they bubbled, I chopped up the meat, and in it went. In a few minutes it turned brown.

"That looks ready," I suggested.

Dan was more cautious. "Better gie it five minutes mair," he said. And we did. The tatties were crunchy and the meat chewy but it must have supplied something we were lacking, for we gobbled it all down. Replete, we tended the fire as the shades of night stole in, and went to bed satisfied.

Dan got up first, complaining of stomach pains. He tried to remove his meal from both corporeal ends and failed, crawling back to his sleeping bag to groan in anguish. Soon I followed him in agony, waiting for the dawn and wondering if it would be our last. Morning found us in the local doctor's surgery, insisting we were emergencies on the point of death. The old man, rather like a real-life Dr Cameron, surveyed us indulgently, "Aye lads, it's a wee bit of food poisoning. I'd stick to the tins till you get back to your mammies."

And he gave us a prescription, in Latin. Our education meant we could read Latin but not his writing, and we waited in the chemist for our salvation. The chemist handed it over and we tore it from its packet outside.

"Syrup o' Figs!" cried Dan in disgust, "I'll stick tae the poisoning." But he did not and it did the trick.

I arrived home with a scar on my palm from opening tins.

This was at Aberfeldy, a place we stuck at for a few days. One reason was that it then had a picture house, the 'Birks', and where there were flics there were floosies. We thought a couple of fast-talking city slickers might manage to impress the local yokelesses, with the tent cast in the role of cupid's couch. We did succeed in escorting a couple, Glasgow keelies on holiday, to the flics and actually sitting beside them after depositing the rusty pennies with the cashier. I remember sitting rigid beside mine while Dan appeared to be engaged in a wrestling match behind. Outside they left us with a flurry of giggles. We analysed the event.

"We were French Kissing," announced Dan.

I had a good idea that this was wicked and decided I could not be upstaged.

"She let me inside her bra," I claimed.

Dan was himself not to be outdone "And I got sticky fingers," he announced.

Whatever this was, I felt obliged to deny that he could have, whereupon an argument ensued that lasted all the way back to the tent. There a lesson in sexual relations was awaiting us. A real one.

In the early 60s there were still many tramps on the road. Not just the tinkers, who you can still see around, but single men tramping. We encountered many. I suppose they were the relics of the vagrants of the Depression, since most of them seemed in advanced middle age. We had been warned by parents against the tramps but around them hung a wild romantic aura; were there not lots of songs about them, bothy ballads about their fine lives?

Come a' ye tramps and hawker lads

That gaes aboot sae braw.

So we were not unduly worried when, at the other side of the railway line to our tent (Aberfeldy had a railway pre Beeching), was a tinkers' encampment. This was the stuff, this was old Ernest Hemingway again! The kids came down to us first; two scruffy lads glowing with health and strength. About our age but products of a different education. We could conjugate latin verbs and use the differential calculus, but they could trap rabbits, guddle for trout and were dextrous with the knives they carried. Our encounters always degenerated into boasting competitions and came close to blows at times.

The woman, a real virago, busied about the camp all day but of the man little was to be seen till evening when he appeared at the fire and started drinking. We were invited to the tinkers' banquet but insisted we had eaten. The man told us, I remember, what to look for in a horse if we ever bought one (maybe he was unimpressed by the bikes). "The teeth," he said, "just like a wife, look at the teeth."

The boys came back, gutted a rabbit they had caught and threw it on the fire to cook. The dogs gobbled up the innards of the rabbit. Fragments of a Nick Adams camp-fire story that turned nasty began to surface in my mind; but that was fiction, this was real life!

The woman, tending the cauldron and the fire, asked us where we had been, where we were going. The man, getting drunker, offered us a drink from his bottle, spittle-greased round the neck. We declined as we had refused the meal and this seemed to annoy him. He persisted and the woman told him to leave us alone. The effect this had on him was astonishing and rooted us to the spot.

From mumbling maudlin drunk he became a fury. He leapt to his feet, knocking over the cauldron, scattering ashes, and threw his bottle at his wife, striking her on the face. We had seen nothing like this even in our low harbour dives. Then he siezed a carving or bread knife and staggered towards her, unsteady on his feet. She ran screaming up the hill behind the camp accompanied by her sons. These in turn produced their knives and brandished them at their staggering father to keep him at his distance. The effort of stumbling uphill in pursuit was his downfall. He collapsed, tried and failed to raise himself, and was soon in the semblance of a coma.

Not a word had passed between us as we watched the scene. The boys brought their father bodily back to the camp and deposited him in the tent. The woman resumed her ministrations. Something was called for, we felt.

"Will we get the police?" Dan asked.

She looked at him as if he were mad. "Police! What for? He does that every nicht. Dinna you go near the police!" she ended, threateningly. She was, and felt, in control. We slunk back to our tent, chastened. In the morning we left early before anyone stirred up by at the encampment.

Thereafter fog obscures the contours of memory again. We emerged from the Highlands back onto roads that had no passing places and whose crowns were not grass-grown, heading back north to Aberdeen. Our last night, I recall, we camped in the Mearns. Flat agricultural country that, then, held little interest for us. It would have later when we discovered Gibbon's *Scots Quair* whose language and politics were ours. Like most adolescents we were amazed whenever we found that someone had previously had the thoughts and feelings we thought were being experienced for the first time in history by ourselves.

The last day we passed by the hospital where I would soon be confined for months, among terminal cancer cases and cretins; where Dan visited me at Christmas and a party got out of hand when he propositioned one of the nurses.

For two years I thought of the mountains we saw on that trip, especially of the 'twelve misty mountains' of the Cuillin seen through the mist in Skye. And two months after throwing away my crutches I was in the Gelder Shiel bothy and on Lochnagar. All that was in the still uncharted future for which I as yet had no map.

We had done over 1000 miles in four weeks, strangers to soap, school and families. Not long after, King Harold would be on the throne, an event treated at our school as comparable to the Fall of Constantinople. Soon black would be beautiful and you could be proud to be a prole. And in the moral loosening of the mid 60s even we managed to lose our sexual innocences.

Back home our ways diverged. Protected by my infirmity I was a licensed jester, never punished, and finished the school, going on to University. Dan sank further and further into malefactions and was soon a shotgun father, bus conductor and later grave-digger. Neither of us wrote the great Scottish novel nor did we manage to change the world (which I, at least, thought would be the easier of the two). We did manage to go to the 'Gorms together and even revisited a much-changing Skye in 1970, for the Cuillin. But eventually we both found maps that took us on separate roads.

It is true, as any reader can see, that we missed a lot. We had no interest in flora and fauna and next to none in the history and culture of the lands we passed through. That summer however was part of a sentimental education which showed us that there was more to life than upward social mobility, even if the wages, the hire of the alternative, was only paid in rusty pennies.

Sex and the Single Bothier

He knew it was not going to work out when she refused to open her eyes on the belay with the poor stance. In that short summer, which in memory will always be sunny, she had proved to be a wonderful companion and hill-walker, scrambling with him over the ridges of An Teallach, the Aonach Eagach and the Cuillin, but she was never going to take to rock-climbing. This was confirmed the next year when they went scrambling in the Dolomites. Caught suddenly on a rib at the edge of a terrifying precipice which only the Dolomites can provide, she, not without reason, turned ashen and froze. Without a rope there was no alternative but to retreat. Rigid with fear, she could only climb down with him below her, his hands on the heels of her boots, guiding her feet to the holds.

There was time, as that relationship crumbled around him, to ponder, as many must have done before him, on the difficulty of the climbing Scotsman in securing a partner who would share his interests. He was aware that for many of his compatriots it was sufficient to have one at home who would tolerate their eccentric behaviour. However in him stirred the embryo of a 'new' man who argued that there must be women of independent mind who would share his passion for the hills.

Perhaps this liberalism was the root of his problems, for this was not the first time he had had difficulties with women. There was the occasion in his younger days when Al had knocked over Jacksonville's big drum full of boiling water onto his foot in a frenzied attempt to usurp his seat beside the young female visitor. Fragments of memory would return from time to time. The pain of his scalded flesh. The desperate midnight crossing of the spateful, waist-deep river, his drunken carrying party so obsessed with keeping the injured limb out of the water that they allowed his upper body to sink beneath. It had seemed in that dark, rain-soaked night that they all might be swept to their deaths. Later, recovering in a Glasgow hospital, there were visits from Al, the girl on his arm. For him? A month to look at the ceiling, and in youthful crassness to think about the perversity of fate and the dangerous role played in it by women. There was no comfort on his return to the climbing scene for he found himself the subject of much hilarity. "I heard a woman made you hot foot it out of Glencoe."

Yet we do not have an answer to our question. Why, in Scotland, in the 60s, did so few women climb? Without much reflection there seems to be a simple answer. There were no women about. The Scottish climbing scene had just never been attractive to them. If it passed through the mind of 60s man at all he would have come up with a simple chauvinistic argument. It would have gone something like this: Among the many burdens which women have to shoulder in their usually subservient relationships with men, is that of attracting a mate. Consequently, although many women will claim that their interest in self-decoration is something they do for themselves, the main purpose is to attract an economically active male who will support them in the manner to which they hope to become accustomed. For this reason women tend to become attracted to activities which a) will ensure meeting a fair selection of the right kind of men, and b) will provide an opportunity to wear some brightly-coloured or fashionable outfit, and where they will not damage their fingernails or get their dangly ear-rings in a twist.

Climbing, despite its super-star television productions and its recent attempts to glamorise things with lycra tights, multi-coloured ropes and anoraks, is not an activity that by and large achieves these ends. Few of the nation's women appear to think that MacInnes, Brown and company are sexy, and the lycra tights soon get dirty and torn after a few struggles with the slippery verticals. Climbing may be a good source of men, but everything else is wrong. (It remains to be seen if the development of competition climbing taking place in comfortable gymnasia, its participants young body-cultured media stars clad in brightly-coloured form-revealing lycra, will change this).

Take for example the weather. Climbing, in even the most benign of climates, suffers from it. Scotland, of course suffers more than most with its midge-ridden wet summers and its Arctic-like winters. Then there is the accommodation. Not for grimpeurs the hotel from which the apres-whatever can take place with the luxury of clean, perfumed bodies and clothes redolent of sexual promise. No, they favour the damp tent, the smaller the better. Or the bothy; four bare walls and no running water, unless it is coming through the roof or from under the door, if there is a door; redolent only of matted sweaty hair, dirty finger nails and arthritis. It is difficult for a girl to look her best under these conditions.

Yet there are women. Women who struggle up a climb often on a tight rope. Or women who are seen staggering under a heavy load ten paces behind their men as they enjoy the delights of Glen Affric. But the cynical amongst us claim to know why they endure. The young man who accompanies them may feel that he has found his ideal partner of bed and belay; someone who only needs a bit of training before she will be able to do really hard climbs. Married, it would be too late to discover she had something else in mind. Into a cupboard will go the boots bought lovingly together in Tiso's. Bothies, once the place of romance, will become smelly holes, unfit for animals. Getting away will become a struggle – it's not fair on the children, there are things to be done around the house. It is no longer worth the hassle to negotiate the time to get away. So the good and the great do fade away.

This picture does women no justice, for as long as there has been climbing in Scotland, women have been involved in their own right and for the purest of motives. Most will have seen the famous picture of Mrs Inglis Clark sitting on Abraham's Ledge during an early ascent of Crowberry Ridge Direct (c. 1904), resplendent in long skirts, hobnailed boots and a large hat attached, no doubt, to her hair by a formidable pin. How calm she looked; she must not have known about the nasty and awkward scoop which waited for her on a climb described at the time as "unjustifiable". There are other, lesser-known, photographs of the same woman starting out on the

On the Cioch

Cioch Slab on Skye, similarly dressed. Even more impressive is the
fact that among the many first ascents in which she took part was
that of Raeburn's Arête (North-east Buttress, Ben Nevis 1902).
Dressed as she was, how did she manage on this climb which was
way ahead of its time? Difficult enough the application of crude
nailed boots to the delicate encrustations which constitute the
majority of holds on this early example of Scottish balance climbing.
But how did she manage to place her feet under those long skirts?
(Since this was written I have been informed that many women of
this period climbed in breeches but carried skirts with them to
present a modest picture when photographed. While this may have
been the case my own feeling is that Mrs. Inglis Clark would not
have felt like wrestling into and out of a skirt on the cramped
Abraham's Ledge for a photograph).

Later, the added hindrance engendered by the desire for feminine
modesty was eschewed by women. By the 1920s the liberating
effects of the Great War were being felt and the mountain dress of
the young flappers of the new Jazz Age was less coy. The long skirts
were being replaced by pragmatic breeches of hairy tweed. And
while the new garments could not be described as sexier than the old
and did not, one suspects, lead to any raised incidence of furtive
fumbling on the belay ledge, at least male partners now knew their
female companions did not suffer from the disadvantages of having
one leg, more or less, than they themselves had. As usual the camera
was there to record these sociological changes, and Humble in his
book, *The Cuillin Of Skye*, has two splendid photographs of two
women, thus coutured, starting and finishing the White Slab Route
without any visible support from a man. The photographs were also
taken by a woman.

Moving on into the 1930s and 40s, women also seemed to figure
in moments of consequence in the climbing life of the marvellous
J.H.B. Bell. He did the first ascent of Eagle Ridge on Lochnagar
with a woman, a route of considerable importance in the development of climbing on Cairngorm granite. This woman was obviously
trusted by the leading climbers of the period for she was the ill-fated

Nancy Forsyth who died so tragically on Ben Nevis with Kellet, despite being warned against climbing with him by Bell. Bell also did early exploratory ascents on the Orion Face on Ben Nevis with a woman. It is interesting to note that he goes out of his way in his book, *A Progress in Mountaineering*, to praise these partners and the ease with which they coped with the difficulties. Was he just being charming (verging on the patronising) as in the style of the time, or was he being honest? I tend to suspect that it must have been the latter, for no better reason than the fact that these women were there and were trusted as seconds at the frontiers of progress. Furthermore it suggested there was nothing intrinsic in the physical or psychological make-up of women of that period which meant they could not climb to the highest standards of the period.

Of course they were seconds, subservient to, and dependent on, male leadership – a reflection of contemporary conventional mores. Their experience therefore was safer, more circumscribed than that of their male counterparts. And for this reason, along with the usual male prejudices, their assistance was not recognised by admission to the Scottish Mountaineering Club, an organisation which, until recently, had remained staunchly single-sexed.

Any hope women may have had for entry into that charmed circle must have died when Bell's generation passed on the torch to W.H. Murray, for there was a dramatic change in the position of women, at least in the literature, of mountaineering in Scotland. They simply disappeared! Murray and his crowd, as far as climbing was concerned, seemed to have had nothing to do with them, for they rate merely two mentions in his books.

This does not mean women were not active in important ways. For example, looking through the old red-bound Scottish Mountaineering Club's guide for Glencoe, one name that catches the eye is that of a Miss E. Speakman who, in September of 1939 accompanied H.I. Ogilvy on the first ascent of Satan's Slit and Red Slab on the Rannoch Wall of the Buachaille Etive Mor. She returned to the same face in January of the following winter with the same partner to do the first ascent of January Jig Saw.

Red Slab is a particularly interesting climb opening up as it did the formidable and blank-looking middle section of the Rannoch Wall. Graded severe in the old book it has given modern leaders anxious moments as they tried to protect with their wee wire nuts the thinnish, steep groove that constitutes the crux. Its modern very severe grading now gives a hint of such difficulties.

But that was then and not the 1960s. It is true that there were women around at this time. There were women in the Langside Mountaineering Club. There was a so-called ladies' doss at Altnafeadh in Glencoe. The Squirrels, always thought to be a right bunch of 'smoothies' in their wee red jerseys, had girl friends, and the phenomenon was not unknown among that most masculine of clubs, the Creag Dhu. However it was during the 50s and 60s that the position of women in climbing, never independent, suffered a sea change the root of which was the dominance of the proletarian mountaineers.

Take a closer look at our odd little group which inherited the proletarian tradition in the 60s. There was some contact with women. Todd had a girl-friend, Big Willie had the occasional success at the dancing in the Glencoe village hall and some even tasted the thrill of a smooch behind Cameron's barn or down by the youth hostel at Lochranza.

But then there was Joe. While many of us were hopeless sex-starved romantics dreaming of camping with yet unmet women in delightful glades found deep in sun-dappled woods, Joe had a more pragmatic approach which, at the time, produced in me feelings of sneaking admiration as well as unease. Paternity suited at eighteen, he was fairly typical of the exploitative male who would fake any emotion, tell any lie to gain cynical advantage over a woman. Thus he would berate us in some tavern where we pumped into timid minds the night's supply of Dutch courage before making one of our rare desperate and predictably unsuccessful forays into Glasgow danceland; the Barrowland, the Magic Stick, the Flaming O. "Ye know the truble wi youse guys? Youse go lookin fur sumwan tae faw in luv wi; sumone tae marry. Well that's no ma style; ah go fur the ugliest wans in the hall. They're that grateful; a couple a times roun the flair, nae problem; know what ah mean?"

Yes, we knew what he meant. Then later; what desperate coupling. The one to satisfy selfish lust, the other trying to please in dark back court or in the underpass of the George VI bridge. A copy of the Daily Record for a bed.

Away the weekends there were few sexual conquests. Only brief little cameos of style. Thus it can be remembered in the noisy glass-clattering, people-chattering, dust-rising through the bars of sun-light in the Aberfoyle, Bailie bar room, Joe necking first with one day tripper then with another. Later, when he surfaced to lick his lips like some contented tomcat he uncharacteristically appeared to offer them some refreshment..."What's youse havin then an that eh?"

"Dubble voddy an tomatta jouse," cooed one.

"Dubble brandy an babysham," fluttered the other.

The barman, a large man, known for his violent maintenance of order applied tumbler to optic while we stiffened, our attention arrested by the unusual generosity. Something was going to happen. We were not to be disappointed.

The drinks arrived as Joe left. As he went he tossed his contempt into the stale pub air. "Yed better pay the man." Like a fuse it produced two explosions. One verbal..."Whadiyameanpaytheman-yameanbastard?" The other, caused by the destruction of the glass thrown at Joe's retreating back. The women's male companions, strangely complacent until then, leapt to their feet to defend their ladies' honour. It seemed like a good time to leave, so we grabbed our packs and hurried out into the dazzling sunshine, to start our march across the Duke's Pass. Frequent glances over our shoulders revealed, to our relief, we were not being pursued.

Apart from Joe's dreadful behaviour, there were other reasons why we did not mix much with women. From their point of view we were not, in the main, an attractive proposition. For a start we were totally dedicated to going away weekends, summer and winter. Not much here to encourage the kind of women who were looking for a nest-builder. Moreover we were, at that time, too deeply immersed in machismo male culture and therefore too bound into that special relationship which young men have that places the opinion of their

mates above all else. What brave woman would have dared compete
with such deep, immature emotions?

And then we drank an awful lot, especially, but not exclusively, on
Saturday nights. It was then one aimed to join the 'Hud' club. So it
was down from the camp-site in the First Glade on Ben A'n; down
through the woods and the twilight of an early autumn evening to the
old stone bar of the Trossachs Hotel where, by the roaring fire one
endeavoured to become a 'Hud' by drinking eight pints of heavy
beer before 'chuckin' out' time at half past nine. Then the drink-
distorted stagger back up the hill, which some never made because
they slid off the path to spend the night down some ravine among the
dying bracken and boulders to wake coldly, gray and rheumy-eyed at
dawn. Not much here to gladden the heart of any intelligent young
woman.

The women we knew, unlike those we had read about, were not
all that active on the hill and therefore not easily integrated into an
outlook dominated by the machismo described above. Why they did
less in the way of climbing than their predecessors can be explained
in a number of ways. Firstly, after the war standards rose ferociously.
The improvement of equipment and the influx of competitive
working-class climbers moved climbing into a new era of exception-
ally steep and strenuous routes which left women trailing in its wake.
Secondly the 60s, for all the emphasis on sexual revolution, was a
nadir for women in their relationships with men. The women of that
decade seem to have fallen between two eras. On the one hand,
while their mothers may have experienced the liberty of wartime
jobs, they had gone quietly back to home and bed to create the baby
booms of the 40s. For that reason perhaps their original sense of
adventure was not something passed on to their daughters.
Moreover the 50s and 60s were, both in society in general and in
climbing circles in particular, the decades of the proletariat. As can
be seen from the behaviour of Joe, women had their place for this
chauvinist group but it was not on the rope on an important first
ascent. On the other hand it was too early for the liberation of the
new feminism of the 70s. As a consequence, like the women of the
30s, most of these women only went on the hill when accompanied

by men. The big difference was that while the women of the 30s climbed in a sense of partnership – albeit as a junior partner – in some of the leading enterprises of the time, by the 60s women were, with some exceptions, reduced to the position of girl-friends or camp-followers.

With the advent of the feminism of the 70s things should have got better. In foreign parts this seems to have been the case. In the USA, women such as Molly Higgins set the pace for the modern females who are pushing close to men. They climb hard in their homeland and have had success on the Himalayan giants. They have their counterparts in France, in Eastern Europe and in England.

But like any other historical movement, its influence is neither complete nor is its progress uniform. Thus high in the Wind Rivers, one can still meet some sun-tanned nymph tossing her blond mane as she murmurs her incantations in praise of her equally sun-tanned and blond climbing hero. He has done this and that, been here and there. She is knowledgeable about severe rock without ever having touched the stuff.

Even at the top end of the market, doubts creep into the mind. Cherie Bremer-Kamp is a case in point. From her book, *Living On The Edge*, the reader cannot but come to the conclusion that she is an intelligent, strong, courageous and resourceful woman, qualities which were required for her winter attempts in alpine style of Himalayan giants. Yet despite the fact that she manifests a feminist consciousness, she reveals that she was embroiled in a most damaging and violent relationship with her lover/climbing partner. In the end he dies high on Kanchenchunga of cerebral oedema and the book, despite his violence to her, is an eulogy to him. So what is one to make of these contradictory passions, the love, and the hate?

One explanation can be offered. Bremer-Kamp was in love with a handsome and brilliant man who was younger than herself. Despite the eulogising the partnership turned out to be fouled with that most ancient form of male/female relationship – the violent patriarch and the adoring woman. She must have known that their relationship could not have endured, and it would be understandable if, in spite of her love for him, she began to fear and despise him. And when he died such emotions could easily turn to guilt and then back to love. The eulogising is thus an atonement for her negative feelings as well as an attempt to freeze forever her original love for him.

Julie Tullis was a lot less complex than the Australian/American, Bremer-Kamp. However, once again from a reading of her book, *Clouds From Both Sides*, the reliance on men for the gifts of life is all too obvious. Although a gutsy climber, when climbing seriously with men she demurs to lead. Later, when during her successful Himalayan experiences she meets an all-women Polish expedition, she notes that such an arrangement would not be for her. Indeed her Himalayan experience and her career as a high-altitude film-maker were almost entirely due to her promotion by the famous Austrian climber Kurt Diemberger, something which is acknowledged in the dedication of her book.

And what of Scotland? Possibilities of a new future have been glimpsed. The future was the young woman who with delicate ease graced the climbing-wall at the Kelvin Hall in Glasgow. Her companion was also female and she bowed to no man. She was as good as any of the young tigers, lacking only their strain. The future was the time we sat beneath the cliff surrounded by mountains of equipment including McGregor's cursed chalk. We had just completed a reasonable enough VS when around the corner she came. Not so young this one. She asked us what we had done and how it was. We answered guardedly knowing what was about to happen. She looked strong and fit; we tried to sit on pieces of gear, thinking – surely we did not need all of this. We did, she did not. She set off up our climb accompanied only by her easy strength. If we had been younger we would have defended our tender egos by degrading her; calling her 'crag hag'. But we were older then and had left behind our confused admiration of men like Joe. We smiled sheepish smiles at each other, packed our gear and went down the hill to think about the changing world. Then there was the young woman in the CIC hut who had, on the afternoon she had walked up with heavy pack, led through with her husband on Bullroar. Equally important, at night in the hut she proved in conversation to be possessed of a personality which did not rely on that of her man.

This is perhaps the crux of the matter: women with men or women with other women, but not women living vicariously through men. Let us not concern ourselves with the sterile debate about whether or not women climbers can ever be as good as men. It seems silly to argue this when there are now good women climbers who are better than most men. As a consequence it may be the moment to raise the banner of liberty and cry 'let the progressive forces of the new woman push away the old order of male reaction! Let the climbing Scotsman's belay and bed be occupied by a truly independent spirit.'

Yet with a moment's reflection the cry dies on our lips. Two truths wither such optimism. The first of these is the nature of the climbing Scotsman himself. Is he ready for such a challenge? Probably not, for his 'independent' woman would have to be someone who would have to do what he wanted to do.

The second, a related and more important truth, lies in the nature of women as they are shaped within our society. The socialisation processes to which both sexes are subjected, and which create not only their different social and psychological states but also, to some extent, their physical state are too complex and too ingrained to be overturned by simply arguing that if only women could acquire independent personalities, they too could be as good climbers as most men. Look around you, the stereotypes still exist. The quiet camp-follower awaits her revenge in matrimony for the humilation of the tight ropes on the climbs beyond her ability, and for the boredom of the endless darts games among the ragged and the smelly. The brash 'bimbo' continues to live vicariously as she drones monotonously on about her man. Women can never be the equal of men in climbing as long as they are subordinate in society as a whole. It is true that as the bonds which have tied women to men in the past have weakened, we have seen the emergence of good women climbers who climb independently of men. However only the socially blind would argue that the process is anything other than just beginning.

The Iron Way: Ticket to Ride

You see them; you see them, frantic. See the turbo-charged fuel-injected hermetic metal boxes they speed out and back in. You see them in the latest gear, heading off in frenzied droves. The menopausal, middle-aged, married men who have discovered Munro-bagging. Men who need an objective at their difficult time in life, but one that fits in with domesticity. They take the kids on Saturday, they get out on Sunday. It is easy to justify for the post-macho man, and easy. No uncertainty, no difficulties bar the walk. In fact, nothing but the walk.

Thinking of the pioneers, 'scaling the tops where foot hath never aforetime trod' (Rev. A.E. Robertson), summons up a different picture. It is true that they did not have the temptation of the car, but one suspects that they were pursuing more than a neurotic, middle-aged impulse. Rather, it was seen as a lifetime's experience, to get to know not only the tops, but the country, its history, its inhabitants.

And was it really that much more difficult for them? Was it just a long haul bred of necessity? The internal combustion engine may not have been much in evidence, but the gentlemen of the SMC could hire steam yachts before 1900 to take them to a Knoydart meet. The railway system was already in existence, allowing Tough and Brown to make their epic attempt at the Ben's North-east Buttress on a two-day trip out from Edinburgh – in 1895; 'after forty-five hours of continuous travelling', they were home. And estate roads gave access to pony and trap, as well as to the ubiquitous two-wheeled pneumatic velocipede. And being gentlemen, which we are not, the pioneers had advantages which we do not. Friendly estates and shepherds provided accommodation, even ghillies to row mountaineers across barriers of river and loch.

Easier or not, the older way was more varied and, one suspects, more interesting and rewarding despite the effort involved. It is not

possible to restore a lost era, but it is possible to take a lifetime, take
it easy. To take a chance, and give the hill a chance. One way of
doing this, is to take the Iron Horse. Great days can be had from the
BR Clydesdale, and on your own wee two-wheeled sholtie.

Single.
To those who abandon the car, and take the train from Glasgow's
Queen Street station, escape begins as soon as pack is deposited on
luggage rack. Before the introduction of the Sprinter trains, the ride
was a rickety one in clapped-out wagons. Slow, allowing the journey
to be savoured, something impossible from the traffic-choked road.
When the line meets the upper reaches of Loch Lomond, the views
of Loch and Ben Lomond are unsurpassed. Further north, Stob
Binnein and Ben Laoigh come into clear and spectacular view. But
the high point of the journey is the crossing, in summer or winter, of
the Moor or Rannoch, conjuring up Eliot's lines,

> Here the crow starves
> Here the patient stag
> breeds for the rifle.
> (*Rannoch by Glencoe*)

Many an ordinary tourist must regard with wonder those descending
at Corrour Halt, a speck on the edge of this wilderness. The thirty-
mile railway loop through the roadless country to the north of Bridge
of Orchy is of great advantage to mountaineers. It opens up country
otherwise very difficult of access, and Corrour is the gateway to this.

Some years ago I descended at Corrour and walked along the
track and footpath to Creaguaineach Lodge by Loch Treig. The
lodge looked abandoned, boarded up. Nearby was an old Land-
rover, looking similarly ownerless but full of salvageable tools. I was
examining these when a grizzled old shepherd appeared from
nowhere. I asked him how long the lodge had been abandoned. He
seemed to consider this carefully. "No, no, it's not abandoned. I'll
be living there." And then he added, with a wry smile, "And that
Land-rover won't be abandoned, either!"

We exchanged pleasantries, and I carried on past the waterfall and through Creaguaineach Gorge, to reach the verdant alp-like pasture above, heading for Stob Coire Easain and Stob a' Choire Mheadhoin.

It had been a hard winter, and it was a late spring, with still little grass showing, though May. Corpses of deer and sheep lay along the path, worried by the foxes, and scattered bones lay as if in a charnel house. Here a sheep was stiffening in its death agony; there a lamb was crawling, new-born, from its mother's slime, the mother too weak to move. Smells of dampness and death assailed my nostrils until I was high on the ridge leading to Easain. The snow was late in melting, and at the summit much evidence could be seen below of recent cornice falls.

I waded, thigh-deep in wet snow, to Mheadhoin, in a biting wind that became fiercer. Low cloud scudded across Loch Treig. It was not a day to linger and I descended back down to the 'valley of death'. From there my route took me westwards to Staoineag bothy, lying two miles furth of Loch Treig. It stands on a lovely knoll across the river from the track through to Fort William. By the time I reached the stepping stones (which I have seen under six feet of water) the evening had improved, and westwards the limpid sunset behind Ben Nevis was striking the top of North-east Buttress.

From Staoineag in the morning, my route took me through the trackless hills towards Glencoe. At Altnafeadh my transport should be waiting. The path skirted a set of ruined shielings, then disappeared southwards into innumerable peat hags. After gaining the watershed, I dropped to the Blackwater Dam, built at the turn of the century to provide hydro-electric power for the aluminium works at Kinlochleven. Below the dam was a shanty town of rude huts. These were built by the men who lived there, summer and winter, and worked, gambled and fought. Their life has been described by Patrick MacGill, in his wonderful book, *Children of the Dead End*,

A sleepy hollow lay below, and within it a muddle of shacks roofed with tarred canvas, and built of driven piles, were huddled together, in bewildering confusion. These were surrounded by puddles, heaps of disused wood, tins, bottles and all manner of

discarded rubbish. Some of the shacks had windows, some had none. It looked as if they had dropped out of the sky by accident.

This was a real bad-lands, where the police went armed to protect the postmen delivering mails, and private vendettas went on outside the law. Some were killed and they lie in the graveyard fenced with wormed wood, containing cheap tombstones flaking with age. There were Poles and Highlanders but most were Irish. Many were only known by nick-names like Black Dan; many had no names at all on their tombstones. Even these were favoured to the many who left their bones whitening on the road to Altnafeadh, returning after drinking sessions at Kings house, and floundering in blizzards.

I passed the rubbish-tip filled with the broken and rusted pots, tools and other rubbish left by the men who tamed the mountain. The path to Altnafeadh was as rough as it had ever been. As rough as it was on the day of the exodus from the Blackwater, when most of the men headed for Rosyth – to build a naval base for a coming war that would take many more of them to their graves. It had been overcast ever since Staoineag and now soft rain began to fall, putting tears on my face for these men. Men who lived and died that you and I might drink from cans.

Mystery Tour.

Sometimes you can see the point of cars, though.

To Inverness was no problem; you left them standing on the A9 as you hurtled north, the bike in the guard's van. No strain, and a meal in the restaurant car, just like a gentleman. Even the transfer into the exhibit of industrial archaeology that was to take you to Bonar Bridge went smoothly. But by then it was drizzling and a long long road, nearly thirty miles of it,

Blackwater Graveyard

lay ahead, up dreary Strath Oykel to Inchnadamph. Why did I insist
on making life difficult for myself?

Along Strath Oykel in pain and bitterness I went. I pedalled one
hour, two hours, three. I was hoping that the weather would worsen,

and pretended not to see the southern slopes of Ben More Assynt as I pulled up to the watershed. In fact the rain was easing off. All excuses for retreat dissolved.

Turning a corner, I stopped and looked west. From thence good weather was being carried in with the evening. The hills of Sutherland – Suilven, Canisp, Quinag – stood in splendid isolation, heads proudly unbowed above the vast sweep of moorland, below the crimson and ultramarine of the sky. Those who have seen this know what I saw, but words cannot convey it to the luckless others. 'Words are dumb.' (Thomas)

I had intended to spend the night at Ledmore, in the biggest AA Box in the world, to which I had a key, courtesy of my wife (a driver). But my drenched state seduced me into a nearby B&B to try to dry out.

They could not have been locals. There was a well-stocked and tended garden. There were goats whose cheese was for sale. There was a woollens workshop. It was 1980, tail-end of the hippie invasion, but before the yuppie invasion. Back to the land; brown rice and kaftans. They were nice. She knitted, he drove the school bus. The locals said they should have kids. There was no one else of child-rearing age in the area, they told me over the home-brewed beer. When the Armenian bean stew arrived, I said I did not mind vegetarianism, really.

In the morning it was wild mushrooms on toast, or eggs; I chose eggs and his face fell. I waited and waited, then looked out of the window. He was chasing a reluctant-looking hen about the yard; he caught it and disappeared into the hen house. I smiled at the squawks, munching my Fru-Grains. When the eggs appeared, I suppressed my desire to change to the mushrooms.

The day was a marvel; a light breeze, sunshine, azure skies. With that and the Fru-Grains I was ready for anything. I took the bike as far up Gleann Dubh as I could, leaving it at a rusted shed. 'Turn your bike loose to browse in the heather, and he will be waiting for you when you return' – the advice of Robertson eighty years ago, I followed.

The path continued up the glen and crossed the river, where it disappeared underground into the Traligill Caves. Then rough tracks led to the col below Conival's shoulder and a scree scramble to the top. I pressed on across the shattered ridge to the summit of Ben More Assynt, there to rest and lunch. What a perfect day! Feeling fit I scrambled on to the south summit before retracing my steps to Conival. There was time for a bathe in the Traligill burn, ice cold, before a leisurely return to the steed.

Consternation, pandaemonium! A puncture! The repair outfit revealed a solution in advanced dessication. Where lay the solution? Lairg thirty miles, or Lochinver eleven? I started to push the offending steed towards the latter.

Doubtless in the afternoon sun the towers of Quinag were resplendent; doubtless Ardvreck Castle on Loch Assynt looked forbidding in shadow. I tried to think about Montrose who was arrested there and later taken and executed at the Grassmarket, but really all I could think of was whether there would be a shop selling cycle tubes in Lochinver. I doubted it. It was a long eleven miles.

There should have been a hitching post. If there had, I would not have been surprised to see mules attached to it. Down an alley off the main street, the corrugated frame bore the legend SUTHER-LAND TRANSPORT AND TRADING COMPANY. It even had a porch on which dogs snoozed. Only the tumbleweed was lacking.

Inside was everything, one supposed, from the needle to the anchor; tins of paint, light bulbs, car spares, tin pails, saws, all in a chaotic jumble. A man with a waist like a Mid-west sheriff was behind the counter; two old men were providing structural support to the same. They stopped talking Gaelic when I came in. It was nearly closing time though it felt like High Noon. I asked if they had bicycle tubes.

"Oh, yess. We'll be haffing them, all right," came the answer.

"Well, can I buy one? Twenty six by one and three eighths."

He looked puzzled by the recitation of numbers, and went into the back room. The old men stared at me, immobile.

The salesman returned with a tube and handed it over. I took it out to check. It would have fitted a child's bike. I prepared to reject it but he would hear nothing of it. "It's the chual messurements now. Efferything is metrificated. Metrificated in inches and...metres!", he ended triumphantly. The old men continued to stare. I went off, went through the motions of stretching, and came back, insisting on a bigger tube. My salesman was clearly upset at the questioning of his expertise in the metric system. But he grudgingly went into the back shop to look anew. The old men stared. I felt there might be a gun in my back.

It was obvious what would happen now. The tube would have fitted the front wheel of a penny farthing. It had probably been there since they were in use. I decided to stand my ground.

"This is no use, it's far too big. I want one twenty six by one and three eighths!"

He assumed a long-suffering superior look, "But it's all the chual messurements now. That Chube dussn't fit in the old messurements, but duss in the new ones."

I went through the ritual. Went outside and came back with the bad news.

"Maybe you could chust be tucking a bit in?" he suggested.

"And maybe I could just be tying the blasted tube in a knot!" I replied in a fury.

He considered this, then replied, "No, that would be stopping the air. Chust be tucking it in. Anyway, we are clossing now."

He waited for us all to go. I stood, motionless. Reluctantly the old men moved away. Once they were gone, and with them the threat of loss of face for him, I suggested, "Look, my bike is very old-fashioned. Maybe if I looked myself I could find a tube?"

He agreed, giving me only a couple of minutes' grace as I rummaged. I found one, thanked him profusely, and paid. The tube said seventeen and sixpence.

"That's two pound fifty," he said, showing his metric knowledge, "but any of the uther chubes would haff done ass well."

Frightened lest he take it back, I agreed, once again blaming my bike, to which I repaired and which I repaired. Only belting back down Strath Oykel, in the lashing rain, did it appear funny.

Week end return
You are always coming back to your starting points otherwise.

> And the end of all our exploring
> Will be to arrive where we started
> (Eliot *Little Gidding*).

But this way there are other possibilities. You can start at
Dalwhinnie and end at Corrour; or start at the latter and end at the
Fort. And there are other options still.

As far as Garve one of the great railway journeys in the world
gives little more than vistas of neeps and rape-seed. But then the
mountains close in, holding the line fast in their grip by Achnasheen.
Twenty years ago I had got off here to spend a marvellous week at
the Ling Hut in Torridon (squatting in the byre while an SMC meet
occupied the hut). The mountains were the oldest in the world, but
we (Stumpy and I) were young and we crossed their shattered ridges
in exultation. The road to Torridon disappeared as the train headed
down towards Achnashellach, the trees closing in on either side.
And the rain too closed in as the glen opened to the west at
Strathcarron. I watched the rain from the platform; it did not look
like relenting.

Shouldering the pack, I began to ascend the path that crossed the
ridge to the west, and led towards Bearnais bothy. It petered out at
the watershed and the mist clagged everything in. By compass I
navigated out of the mist and descended to the doss below. It had
been a foul summer; the ground was wet, the going hard, the
vegetation luxuriant. It was almost dark as I unpacked but I could
just read the memorial to 'Beardie' – Eric Beard – in the bothy; the
man who still held the Cuillin Ridge record at that time, running it
in less than five hours. I had little hope for the morrow as I settled
down.

Clammy, oppressive, but the cloud above the tops as I set out.
Fording the Bearnais river, and threading through the peat-hags and
rutted coarse grass produced profuse sweat and curses; bluebottles
irritated the life out of me. But as if by magic, a stalkers' path
appeared that carried me far up the mountain side, to where I could

see the shoulder of Bidein a' Choire Sheasgaich steepening ahead. Not quite the remotest hill in Scotland, but Lurg Mhor which lay at the far end of an adjoining ridge, probably was and I hoped to ascend them both that day.

Like most shapely, grassy hills, Bidein was more interesting to look at than ascend. From Lurg Mhor it looked spectacular, but the actual ascent was an unrelieved slog up wet grass and boulders, sweat running into my eyes. A big descent and equally big pull up over slabby rock led to Lurg Mhor's summit and an unexpected bonus in the rocky scramble along to the Meall Mor top. The crags here looked as if they might offer scope for first ascents.

East and south of me lay the lands described in *Isolation Shepherd*, a book I had just read, by Iain Thomson. A book which idealised the life of the great estates before they were 'spoiled' by the hydro and the forestry – which brought more work and prosperity than the landlords ever did. The very landlords who had evicted the inhabitants to create the paradise whose passing Thomson laments, and who were compensated to the hilt for their losses. Do not lament the passing of Lachan the Lackey and Dochan the Dope.

Turning back towards Lurg Mhor I encountered another walker at the summit in a state of near exhaustion. No wonder: he had walked from Achnashellach and had now to retrace his steps. I told him I had taken two days so far and would walk out the next, to complete the hill. He looked surprised and sceptical, "But the book says it can be done in a day!" he corrected.

Which book, I could tell. The bible of the day-outers, the car-parkers, the frenzied ones. I escorted him back to Bidein, whence he headed off at a snail's pace for the Bealach Bhearnais. I dropped to the welcoming sight of the bothy, empty.

The mist had again descended the next day. I ascended the burn behind the bothy and at the misted summit, again relied on compass to guide me down to Achnashellach, via a miniature rocky defile like something from the Afghan frontier. At the river cows stood in the stream. I judged it thus safe and forded to gain the deserted platform at Achnashellach. Fuar Tholl was veiled in black, like a woman in mourning. The rhododendron leaves hung wet, their flowers faded. I waited for the train.

Day return.

And you can fit a bit of romance even into a married man's day, one of those days when some dreadful Meall a' Bumpy awaits your reluctant feet and rationed time.

The delightful fretwork, in hues of green, of Bridge of Orchy station loomed and I went to the guard's van to get the bike. The train stopped and I opened the door. The platform was twenty feet away, the ground six feet below me. I might have contemplated a hobo descent – but not with the bicycle. I raced through the train and leapt out, hauling down the guard's green flag and almost making him swallow his whistle, before persuading him to run the train forward for my descent.

And away. Over the old Caulfield military bridge and the old road to Glencoe. Past the Caledonian pines fringing Loch Tulla, and Inveroran Hotel where the SMC had early meets, its first members snapped below the porch, I speeded past. The next bridge crossed the Allt Tolaghan, which flowed from a glen where Duncan Ban MacIntyre, the great Gaelic poet, had been born. My father-in-law with a load of bodachs from the Inverness Gaelic Society had staggered up there recently under the weight of a memorial to Donnachy Ban. And then, matching the poet's own achievement when over seventy, had climbed Beinn Dorain. The Glenorchy Shepherd must have been one of the first Scottish mountaineers, climbing Beinn Dorain in the late eighteenth century – possibly that mountain's first ascent. He wrote of the experience thus,

> The precedence over all mountains goes to Beinn Dorain, I think it the most beautiful I have seen under the sun.

If the bodachs could do Beinn Dorain I can surely do Stob a' Choire Odhair, I thought; another of those hills I had missed in the days when I only did the interesting ones. I reached the GUMC hut, formerly the schoolhouse for the region, and chained the bike to it. A friend of mine had assured me that the hut 'was bigger on the inside than on the outside'. As I looked at its tiny dimensions I thought it would have to have this miraculous feature to be any use

BEN MORE
ASSYNT

BONAR BRIDGE

ACHNASHELLACH

LURG MHOR

INVERNESS

KYLE

AN SCARSOCH

TARF BOTHY

SGURR NAN
COIREACHAN

GLENFINNAN

CORROUR

BLAIR ATHOLL

BLACKWATER
DAM

BEN DORAIN

GLASGOW

Iron Way: Ticket to Ride

as a club hut.

As usual, it was not so bad. A pleasant walk up the Allt Toaig by wood and pool and, once the higher ground was reached by an easing stalkers' path, the views over the Rannoch Moor compensated for the uneventful nature of the walk. But as I looked at the corries and ridges of Stob Ghabhar, there was still something perverse in being where I was.

No one had rustled the bike at the hut, and I was soon back at Bridge of Orchy; but it was three hours before a train would be there. Browsing over the noticeboard, I noticed that a train would be at Dalmally, on the Oban line, in two hours. It was fourteen miles, downhill. Down Glen Orchy, where Donnachy Ban had shepherded – and at Dalmally there was another monument to him. Looking at the fine cone of Beinn Dorain I felt I owed him this.

It was largely free-wheeling down Glen Orchy, by the wooded river, interrupted only when a daft tourist flagged me down, to pull him across one of the bucket bridges and take a picture of him over the flow. I declined his offer to do the same for me.

A back road from Dalmally took me in two miles to the monument, an ugly memorial but a good viewpoint over Loch Awe and Campbell country. The first man to climb Beinn Dorain, Duncan Ban was a Campbell dependant. He was enlisted against the Jacobites in 1745, but deserted; whether from Jacobite sympathies, or self-preservation, is not known.

> The precedence over all mountains goes to Stob a' Choire Odhair...

No, it did not have the same ring to it.

Standard return.

One of the recurrent topics of conversation amongst bothiers and mountaineers is the 'Great Last Wilderness Debate', with Knoydart and the Fisherfield Forest being much favoured candidates. But watching Knoydart disappear under holiday homes and never having seen fewer than 50 people at the Fisherfield's Shenavall bothy, I aver that neither area can compare with the land around the headwaters

of the Tarf. It is true that this area cannot compete with its rivals in
scenic drama; low rounded hills roll repetitively to the horizon in all
directions, featureless and trackless. But that very fact of topography
contributes to the sense of isolation. And when to this is added that
the famous 'Tarf Hotel' (a semi-ruinous shooting lodge at almost
2000 ft) is a full fifteen miles from Blair Atholl, Linn o' Dee, or Glen
Feshie, then it is clear that all rival claims to be the 'last wilderness'
in Scotland must be spurned in favour of the hills around the source
of the Tarf Water.

    To end one summer's holidays on a high note I decided to see the
Tarf again. My preferred route is by Blair Atholl, since you can
shorten the walking by taking a bike in the train. A mere couple of
hours out of Glasgow and you are heading up the rough track to the
head of Glen Tilt. The Tilt ascends by deep pools and turbulent
gorges through the landscaped area around Blair Castle, then
through mixed natural and planted woodlands, to emerge into the
steep reaches of the upper glen. This glen was the occasion of a
famous access case fought in 1847 against the Duke of Atholl by a
group of Edinburgh botanists. Their success was commemorated in
the 'Battle of Glen Tilt',

                    Twas a' tae poo
                       Some gerse that grew
                    On Ben Muich Dhu
                       That ne'er a coo
                    Would care to pit her moo till.

My trusty 'minister's bike' (no terrain-chewing mountain bike this
one) made short work of the first ten miles or so, and in a little over
an hour after detraining, the iron steed was abandoned at a pony
shelter high on the moor. The rest of the distance to the 'Hotel' (so-
called from the metal AA signs at the door) was done on foot and
there is little in the way of a track. In the more than five years since I
had seen it there had been much further deterioration in the bothy;
the estate declines to carry out, or to allow, maintenance – possibly
wishing to discourage visitors from what is prime deer country.
There was evidence, nevertheless, of increasing use in the form of

the mass of bottles and tins littering the collapsed outworks of the building. Doubtless this pleased the wee moose that tamely scampered over the floor foraging for scraps of food from my meal.

The Tarf is deer country. Already the stags in their russet coats seemed hyper-nervous, as if aware of the approach of the shooting season. They filed away over the heather next day as I walked en route to Carn an Fhidhleir and An Sgarsoch. On the top of the latter I noticed the rude remains of the enclosures dating from the times when a horse market was held on its summit. On descent I also noticed what was everywhere evident that year; a plague of puddocks, like that which visited Egypt in biblical times. I was further pleased to see a couple of dippers, bobbing like obsequious waiters in the burn. Their numbers are declining, owing to loss of food supplies from acidification of the burns. On the hills themselves though, no one, despite the marvellous day.

On the way out a hair-raising, brake-testing descent from the Tarf to the Tilt took me past the ruins of old shielings, where menial formerly tended bestial. Visions of tea and scones and a dram in the Blair Atholl pub formed as I sped down the track. Even the unmistakeable evidence of a flat tyre did not bother me, as I had been foresighted enough to pack a spare tube. But my smugness was punctured when I realised I'd forgotten the spanner. Past Forest Lodge, with seven miles to go and a train to catch, I noticed a fisherman with a Lada and my mind turned to its famous tool kit. But alas, the newest model is supplied with only pump and jack and I trudged on.

Then across the river at Balaneasie – a club hut – I spied a lad chopping wood. Did he have a spanner? Nae bother, and it was strapped to the wooden seat of a pulley bridge and hauled over the torrent. In a trice the tube was replaced and the spanner dancing its way back over the river; the bridge looked as if anything heavier than the spanner would drag the whole structure down into the water. Pedal progress was resumed and I made the train.

There was time for the tea and scones but not the dram.

Rail Rover

An excess of hobo tales from Steinbeck and Hemingway at a tender age is a bad thing. Though you know it's not there you keep looking for the cattle truck, the camp-fire and the songs.

I had high hopes. I had even bought a collapsible fishing rod to go with my five-day railpass. The weather had been good, you see, but as we approached the white man's graveyard of Fort William the drizzle started. Nothing daunted, I descended at Glenfinnan station with the bike, and proceeded to prepare for my journey. Bad omens were accumulating; the bike was locked and I had forgotten the key. A hacksaw borrowed from the first house removed that problem but not the feeling that this trip was to go astray.

Pedalling under the concrete railway arch, I shuddered up the glen to arrive at Corriehully bothy; twenty minutes, instead of the usual hour and a half, I thought smugly.

An hour later the heavens opened and the wind rose.

Neither stopped for thirty six hours. All that night, the next day, and the next night it came down in sheets. The river rose from a trickle to overflow its banks. I peed from the step and collected rainwater to cook, not stepping outside all that time. I was beginning to feel like Noah facing the flood. The next morning again it had lifted a little. Cabin-fever having set in, I started off for Sgurr nan Coireachan. I had company. The previous night a camper, swept from his tent, had arrived in a state of semi-hypothermia and he came along for the walk.

We walked up the glen, chatting as people do, noting the efforts to plant deciduous trees that were being made on the slopes. Low mist followed us to the top of Sgurr nan Coireachan but on the descent to Sgurr Thuilm it cleared, giving views of Knoydart to the north and the Small Isles to the west. The ridge was a pleasant walk of character. Coireachan is shapely and slabby but Thuilm a big lump. We lunched at a small lochan, noticing a dwarf rowan tree at 2800 ft, and parted at Sgurr Thuilm. He was off into Knoydart.

The bothy looked uninviting on my return. There was nothing more to burn and I was short of supplies, so I high-tailed it back down to Glenfinnan. The pub provided food and liquid refreshment, the railway waiting-room an unexpectedly luxurious doss. Pine-pannelled, and with an electric wall heater; even running water available in the toilet down-platform. Despite half my doup hanging off the bench, I slept the sleep of the just.

Morning saw me back in Fort William with a couple of hours to kill before the train home. A trip to the swimming pool and sauna solved that problem. Sadly, my residual romantic hoboist feelings were stirred at Tulloch, when it looked as if the 'Lochaber sunshine' was going to stop pouring down. Out I jumped and hastened towards Beinn Teallach and Beinn a' Chaorainn, leaving my gear in the station. For about two hours it was pleasant. On the ascent of Beinn Teallach's easy slope, I saw and heard a couple of Golden Plovers. It was going to be a good day...

Half-way back up from the col between the two mountains the monsoon started, and a chilling wind got up. Visibility declined to near zero and the compass came out. It was summer, officially, and I was lightly clad. If I had stopped I am certain I would have got hypothermia. As it was, a numb hand held the compass till I regained, after a battle through sodden pines, the bike. I could hardly feel the handlebars so dead were my hands to sensation. As the rain continued to pour down, it occurred to me that this was not a climate to hobo in.

But again I was saved by the Iron Horse. The waiting-room had a fireplace and by various environmentally-friendly depredations I managed to get enough timber to start a blaze and dry off. No hobo ever had this luxury. An electric light, a settee long enough to stretch the sleeping bag out on, and a flush toilet and sink with tap in an annex. And I was sure Tulloch did not have a vigilante citizen's committee to run the likes of me out of town, after a good tarring and feathering.

On the way home in the train next day, the horrors of it all were already fading. By the time I wrote up my hill log it had assumed a rosy glow. Maybe I will get to use that fishing rod yet.

So was it harder in the good old days? I'm not so sure. When I read of Inkson-McConnochie easing the ascent of Ben Macdhui in winter by the use of a horse-drawn sledge from Braemar to Derry Lodge – in 1890 – or of Inglis Clark (despite his only too firmly-grounded fear that 'motor driving will cause a degenerate race of mountaineers to arise') in 1903 describing a motor mountaineering tour in Glencoe and Nevis, I'm inclined to be sceptical. None of them ever, I suspect, had the delight of being turned unceremoniously off a train at Arrochar at midnight (it having previously broken down at Crianlarich), to face a thirty-five mile cycle back to Glasgow on a velocipede that lacked artificial means of illumination. My proletarian solidarity with the striking railwaymen, fighting to save their jobs and the line, was much needed as I rode

> I' the how-dumb-died o' the cauld hairst nicht
> (MacDiarmid *The Eemis Stane.*)

And is it worth it? Here let us hear the man who started it all. Robertson again,

> "Peak-bagging...(is), I fear, somewhat looked down upon...What delightful weeks I have spent in this manner...I look back upon the days I have spent pursuing this quest as among the best spent of my life. Amid the strange beauty and wild grandeur of rock face and snow slope...he would be indeed dull of heart who could see and feel that unmoved." (SMC Journal 1902).

And who am I to gainsay a man of the cloth?

The Sound of Knuckles on Flesh and Other Forms of Bad Behaviour

As the bus pulled into the side of the road its tyres grated on the gravel. Inside the noise was that of empty bottles, clinking as they rolled together on the cluttered floor. Ronnie surveyed grimly the scene at the back of the bus. Among the bottles lay the bodies, bedecked with sickness: the result of drinking the contents of the bottles. Five hours from Glasgow to the Lake District and they had to get drunk. He blamed that wee red-headed one at the back, the one with the quick line in patter. He could not get them out the pub until closing time and Red there had brought all that cider from the Sarry Heid to sell en route. The innocents had gobbled it up. They'll never make it to Styhead Tarn, he ruminated bleakly, never mind get a day's climbing in tomorrow.

No one at the back of the bus stirred until the sober were ready to leave. It was about four in the morning by then. "How farsit to this Styhead Tarn place then Ronnie?" slurred a figure as he rose unsteadily from the debris. "Too far for you lot," came the terse reply. The figure, as if to confirm this verdict, slumped back onto the damp seat. That, as they say, seemed to be that. And yet this was red rags to these bulls – the hardest boys in the club. With time they would respond.

And respond they did. Slowly at first. Brains still befuddled by their over-indulgence, they got their gear together and started down the road. Then faster as the adrenalin of the chase took hold. Was this not what they were used to? The hard walks, drunk or sober, day or night, winter or summer. All the better if there was competition. Had they not destroyed Lord Hunt's golden boys, scattering them over the Cairngorms when some were foolish enough to resent being passed by Glasgow scruff? Or there was that time when Bugsy and his Squirrelly crew tried to steal a march on them by spiriting themselves away through the Distillery to get first to the workman's hut which used to stand beside the Allt a' Mhuilinn at the entrance of the corrie of cold Ben Nevis. They had passed them, left them exhausted on the brow of the hill with a few hundred yards to go: to the victors, the dubious comforts of a tin hut with no door, high on mid-winter Ben Nevis; to the losers, to watch the smooring sleet gather round the eaves of the damp tent.

But this time no such level of ease was achieved. For once the sober had been left behind in the dark night and fog, the adrenalin was overwhelmed by alcohol, tiredness and disorientation. The solution – to bed down among the bogs if a dry spot could be found. In the morning, there was much hilarity to be had at the expense of Peter, asleep on a steeply-angled boulder, his sleeping bag at his waist, his position sustained only by hanging on to the upper edge of his inhospitable stone in the manner climbers call a lay-back. In the face of adversity, survival is achieved by the instinctive use of training.

They may not have made Styhead that night but they did climb that day. It was not with the usual enthusiasm, energy and style that would, in later years lead some of them to the doors of sacred Jacksonville and entry into the Creag Dhu. So while Ronnie, grim-faced and showing that he could still do it (even though none denied that he could) stressed his way up the innocently-named but nasty Buttonhook, they scraped around the bottom of the crags, heads thick and bodies listless. For those who did climb there was the possibility of being sick at the bottom, middle and top of slippery Kern Knotts Crack. However it was not only the effects of the travel sickness of the previous night that produced this indifference to the delights of the English climbing scene. There was a darker reason that lurked deep in the recesses of a consciousness made brittle by national pride.

Like many of their compatriots, without thinking very much about it, they held in contempt all things English. To show enthusiasm for their climbs would be as meaningful as to appreciate English football and their winning of the World Cup. They had been at Wembley when Baxter had destroyed them; had danced in the streets and fountains of their capital. Generations of perceived slights, real or imagined, required many such dances. Such is the foolish behaviour of the dispossessed, the powerless. Apart from the feeling of celebration for the kind of long holiday weekend required to get to the Lakes – in these days before dual carriageways – to come to England was not to climb but to indulge in a ritualistic denial of English superiority. That night, down at the Wasdale Hotel, there would be another dance of denial.

Such an event would start off quietly enough – after a few drinks the guitars would come out. They were not bad singers so the crowd were happy enough at the thought of some free entertainment. However it did not stop there and as the night wore on the Scots' behaviour became more and more boisterous. The songs would become rude and get ruder. Young women, despite the close attentions of their boyfriends, would find themselves the target of amorous advances. The puzzled look on Pharaoh, the large Cumberland-wrestling proprietor of the time, became even more puzzled as he threw out the odd Scotsman only to see him brazenly re-enter the pub a few minutes later with his hair combed a different way and his collar turned up. Pharaoh was not fooled. Just tired of throwing out silly Scotsmen.

The English, safe in the security of their sober superiority, could not understand such perversity and they watched in puzzled silence as the over-refreshed Scots sang and fell about drunkenly. Later in the barn as the Scots continued with their orgy of self-destruction, the English slipped away leaving the field to the vanquished.

In such behaviour there is little to be proud of and in retrospect it seems strange that it did not invite the retribution of a punch-up. Indeed, despite all the myths that have grown up over the years about the hard men of Scottish climbing, there was little in the way of actual violence during the 50s and 60s. Consequently, although they suffer through lack of a violent climax, the stories related below are a closer representation of the true nature of this era than tales of mythical rough-houses. It is true that one heard of tough characters like the Creag Dhu man who took to living in a northern English

town. It seems that in his youth he was so small and inoffensive-
looking, the local hard-cases would try to take a rise out of him. To
their shock and horror his response was devastating. Off would
come his glasses and he would weigh-in with his arms flailing
around their faces. His famous finish to the combat was to stick his
fingers up his tormentors' noses and pull in an upward fashion. At
this point his friends would drag him off.

But he was unusual. More typical was the show-down which
relied on a cool head out-psyching would-be belligerents. The
sources of these conflicts were many and confused. International
and city rivalry, competition between leading lights, as well as
traditional tensions between the town and the country were
aggravated by the normally aggressive behaviour of young males.

We have already seen how it operated on an international level.
Witness now conflict between the town and the country.

Once there was a young man who spent his winter weekends on
Ben Nevis. In those days, before the ark and before the Terrordac-
tyl, this was the province of the few. Despite his youth he had done it
all, or at least most of it. He had crouched under the ice-bulge on
steps of his own construction, his arm muscles aching as he
fashioned his salvation with his axe before darkness or spindrift
engulfed him. With the wind rattling the ice in his incipient beard,
he had balanced on his ice-axe plunged into hard snow beneath the
huge cornice, and above a void unimaginable to the layman, his
cold-stiffened fingers trying to gain some purchase on the glassy
surface. He had followed the flickering needle of the compass down
through mist and dark and howling gale, through the grasping jaws
of the ice-mantled cliffs to the warm sanctuary of the CIC hut.

Yet not content with these dangers he decided to challenge the
local worthies in the toilet during a dance in Fort William's hall.
Shunning the delights of the dance floor these loyal subjects of her
majesty had retired to the smelly auditorium, there to sing a
collection of well-known songs of the Protestant religious persua-
sion. They included such favourites as the one about their father
wearing a strange garment that was coloured orange, as well as the

one that cheerily told of the joy of being up to one's knees in Fenian blood. Our lad was not particularly offended by this, but thought, in the interests of fair play, the other side should get their turn. Accordingly when they had ceased their celebrations of 1690 in order to refresh their thrapples with a delicate swig at a half bottle, he lifted his head back and gave a very passable rendition of Sean South of Garry Owen. Unfortunately the locals did not share this sense of balance. They did not suppose their ancestors had spilled blood fighting the rebel James so that they could be confronted by the enemy in their own toilet. Thus they began to advance menacingly towards the songster. It did not look good.

Then, just as the violence was about to begin, there was, from the direction of the door, the sound of glass against· stone. All heads jerked towards the door as if pulled by one string. There, in the doorway, the jagged edge of a broken bottle in his hand, its contents oozing round his feet, was Way Back Jack (so called because he always started his stories with "Way back..."). He looked real mean as he eyed each man with a steady steely blue eye. In the silence created, Way Back spoke very slowly and very precisely. This was not a moment to lose the effect. "If yere gonnae have him yere gonnae have tae have me first."

The result was shattering, for although they outnumbered the Glasgow lads, the bold boys of the toilet declined to take up Way Back's invitation and in surly silence they slunk back to the dance where large numbers of climbers ensured they could take no action to salve their wounded pride.

Arran was another place in which the locals could prove difficult. It was the custom of the times for young Glasgow climbers to join the throngs of Glasgow University students in their annual celebration of the end of summer by invading that island. It was all innocent fun. Hordes of young people crowded together on trains bound for the Clyde coast where they would board the ferries to Arran. The scenes in the various small ports could be fantastic. There would be small ferries whose alarming list towards the pier was caused by the enthusiasm of the crowds which lined one side of the boat to greet their friends as they came aboard. In the stern there could be a jazz band playing and, despite the crowds, couples dancing. In imitation of the streamers thrown at the departure of the large transatlantic liners, the occasional toilet-roll would unwind itself through the night sky. Once there was an outrageous piece of behaviour that necessitated police intervention. Someone had taken down the red duster at the stern and replaced it with a Soviet flag. In those less sophisticated times, the crowd gasped at such political audacity.

Once on Arran there did not seem much to do. An overcrowded dance on Saturday night in the Brodick village hall, or an attempt at a sausage fry on the beach was about the extent of it. For most it was a weekend of drinking in the local bars when they were open and a miserable walk around in what was often wet weather when they were closed. No wonder come early Monday morning the bedraggled campers were retreating from Glen Rosa like some defeated Jacobite army to catch the first ferry back to the mainland.

The climbers were, of course, made of sterner and wiser stuff. They eschewed the crowds of Glen Rosa and the students in Brodick and made their way by bus and foot to quiet Glen Sannox. There they would camp in wooded glades convenient for climbing on Cir Mhor.

Often the target the next day was to climb on the beautiful granite Rosa Pinnacle of Cir Mhor. A favourite climb was the South Ridge Direct with its delightful variety of pitches on perfect rock. The most memorable of these is the overhanging Y Crack pitch where the climber's lunge for the two breast-like holds at the top is often hampered by his foot being jammed in the crack. Many a bold young climber has had a disturbing vision of himself hanging upside down attached only by this jammed foot.

However, like our friend in the Fort William toilet, these were men possessed of an excess of energy and they also looked to the delights of the Saturday night dance. So after a day on the slabs of the South Ridge, or more uncomfortably on crumbly climbs like Ruddy Knuckles or Prospero's Peril, the lads would take a quick dip in the burn before setting off for the hotel in Corrie. Their plan was

Bad Behaviour

as follows: a few drinks in Corrie before taking the bus down to Lochranza – a few more drinks there, a telephone call to book a local taxi for the journey back to Glen Sannox, before buying a big carry-out for the dance in the local village hall.

All this was achieved without difficulty. Problems only arose when they tried to gain entry to the dance. At the entrance to the hall they were met by some big local lads who said that they could not take their carry-out into the dance with them. While there were some mumblings of discontent about this uncivilised arrangement, the Glasgow boys agreed to be separated from their precious cargo of drink.

The dance was grand. The band struck up. The accordion squealed and the drums rattled. The reels were reeled, the jigs jigged. In favoured Strip the Willow, lassies were flung around the chalk-dusted floor to the accompaniment of loud hoochs. They squealed in delight, their skirts flowing behind them as they birled and spun from one strong arm to another. All in all it seemed a great success and some of the Glasgow boys even managed to walk girls back to the Youth Hostel, where there was time for a quick smooch before returning to the hall to catch the taxi back to Glen Sannox.

It was then the trouble began. Outside the hall, their figures illuminated by the backlight of car headlights, a tight little knot of people had collected. Around this was gathered a larger, looser group. The inner knot consisted of two groups. Locals – big lads – said later to have come from Corrie, white shirted and jacketless despite the chilly autumn night, their large arm muscles shown off to good effect by shirt-sleeves rolled up as far as they could go. And some of the Glasgow boys – smaller – for many were of Irish descent and their bodies and faces were marked by the deprivations of the race. Used to the outdoors, they were more appropriately clad in their uniform of combat jacket, baseball boots, jeans with the regulation four inch turn-ups and eight piece bunnets.

Even to the most casual onlooker it was obvious that all was not well between the locals and their visitors. All the usual signs of incipient combat were there. Bodies were set rigid, gestures were short in movement, hands raised to make some point, heads moved in agitation. The condensed breath from their open mouths steamed into the night air. The problem was the carry-out – it had disappeared and the Glasgow boys sniffed betrayal. Thus the accusations and denials passed to and forth until the inevitable hiatus was reached.

From the outer looser, more relaxed group came a man. A man of honour, a peacemaker no doubt. He stepped between the two antagonistic groups and announced that he, the peacemaker, was a special constable. This, he probably thought, would bring a sense of proportion to the combatants and calm things down a little. He could not have been more wrong, for as soon as he announced his honorary title, one of the Glasgow boys pushed forward to hit him with such precision that he dropped instantly to the ground, where he wisely remained to take no further part in the proceedings.

Why had his honourable intentions failed so spectacularly? The problem was, you see, that his attacker had earlier that year been

arrested in Fort William for some minor misdemeanour and had not
wanted to repeat the unfortunate consequences of another arrest. So
he hit him! A peculiar logic some may think – but a logic
nevertheless.

Anyway no sooner had the crowd recovered from the sight of the
peacemaker hitting the ground than two things happened almost
simultaneously. The first of these was predictable – the exchange of
words degenerated rapidly into an exchange of blows. The second –
the one which saved the Glasgow boys – was the arrival of the taxi
hired to take them back to Glen Sannox. Into this they gratefully
retreated, all the time fighting a spirited rearguard action.

The white-shirted locals, dismayed no doubt to be robbed of their
prey, surrounded the taxi urging the driver, whom they seemed to
know, to give up the Glasgow scruff. But he too was an honourable
man – a peacemaker, and a more successful one than the special
constable, now to be seen to the rear nursing sore pride and a sorer
nose. Disdaining to lose his handsome fare that night, he eased his
car away from the locals and with a crunch of tyres on gravel sped
towards Glen Sannox.

The locals, not wanting to lose their sport, jumped into their cars
and gave chase. And travelling much faster than the careful taxi-
driver they were not long in catching and passing the Glasgow boys.
It was not an encouraging sight. To them it seemed that every closed
window of the pursuing cars was occupied by a snarling face, while
through every open window waved a large and threatening fist.
There could only be one conclusion – a large and bloody ambush at
the mouth of Glen Sannox.

Joe, a street-fighting man to the end, surveyed calmly the red
lights of their tormentors disappearing into the damp darkness
ahead. He knew what to do for during the mêlée outside the hall he
had slid into the building to recapture the carry-out. "Here boys,
have a screwtap each. That'll sort these mugs out." With skill and
courage they might survive the night. He was not, however,
encouraged as to the outcome when he noticed that some of the
younger, more naive members of the small band did not appear to

know whether they were meant to hit people over the head with the bottles or drink their contents. "Youse want tae get your fuckin' act together!" he said through clenched teeth so as to impart the seriousness of their situation.

It was quiet – too quiet, as they say in all the best pictures – when they arrived at Glen Sannox. The road was empty save for the moonlight which was reflected on the damp tar surface. The boys, screwtops in hand, eyed nervously the hedges and bushes which could hide a regiment of locals ready to spring forth. But as they stood in that night, darkness ebbing and flowing as the moon passed from cloud to cloud, nothing stirred.

Then suddenly, from the direction of Brodick came the sound of squealing tyres. The boys tensed, each one feeling the screwtop in his hand as though measuring its weight and balance. Soon they may have to crack heads with them. Funny though, the thought trickled through the back of each mind, while several cars had passed them that night as they left the village there was now only one car.

It stopped directly across the road from the boys and just in front of the single house that stood in those parts. The boys grew even more apprehensive. What was going to happen now? As it turned out – not a lot. A girl got out of the car, leant back in to kiss the driver before standing up to see the group of desperadoes gawking open-mouthed at her. She squealed in fright before running into the house.

The boys walked up the glen, their emotions mangled. They had stepped into a conflict which was not of their choosing for it seems that every year the local lads picked on a crowd from Glasgow to demonstrate that they were the toughest. This mattered little to the climbers whose relief at getting away without a fight was covered by the vain fantasies of the battle which never really was. Proud boasts rang out through the chilled autumn night. "Just as well they never showed up; we would a fuckin murdered them. Natrightannateh?" Nevertheless when they returned from the hill the next day, the camp was entered cautiously, just in case the local hard cases had indeed showed up.

Have you ever witnessed the clash of giants? The real-life

Dangerous Dan Magrews. The men who are the stuff of myth. This story concerns the non-violent conflict between two such men. The first was a man of the Creag Dhu – a quiet man, a man who seldom spoke but who commanded so much respect that when he did, people listened. The second was a famous English climber. Some might have described him as the original 'ard man, famous for his unathletic girth, flat cap, drinking and fighting exploits, brilliant climbing innovations and, latterly, Himalayan triumphs. They were among the merry revellers who had gathered together to celebrate the forthcoming nuptials of another member of the Creag Dhu at the Loch Ard Hotel in the Trossachs. As was the custom of such a gathering it was all male. However the company had been joined by some others who happened to be there and who had among their number some women, as well as a man who played a guitar.

The proceedings also had a traditional shape about them for along with a great deal of drinking there was a tendency to sing songs that became ruder as the night went on. The guitar player had began to annoy our quiet man by constantly trying to impose his musical tastes on the company, when the Englishman suddenly said something which surprised everyone. "I think we should have less of the dirty songs. After all there are ladies in the company." The quiet man leant over and poked a stubby finger in the Englishman's chest. "See you," his voice pregnant with violence. "Any more from you and you're going out that window – followed by that guitar player." The strumming of the guitar dwindled out and the Englishman did not respond. It was like a goal being scored against the English but without the Hampden roar.

Clashes between climbers were not restricted to international rivalry, for the Scots have always managed to squabble among themselves. In the 60s there was intense competition between the Creag Dhu and the Squirrels. This came to head one summer when John Cunningham, who had just got off a boat from Antarctica, failed on some climb on the Etive Slabs. Tongues wagged, for often climbers are no better than old wives, and rumour had it that Bugs, a prominent Squirrel, was going around telling all who were foolish

enough to listen that Cunningham was finished. Whether or not
Bugs was actually indulging in such talk, has long since slipped into
the equivalent position in the oral history of Scottish climbing, as
that held by the discussion regarding the number of angels who
could balance on the head of a pin.

Rumour or not, pride was hurt and Cunningham responded with
an invitation to Bugs to discuss the matter in the twilight of a
beautiful Scottish evening outside the Kingshouse. There were no
blows – just some finger gestures and denials and that was the end of
it. Later when the Creag Dhu were scattered to the winds
(Cunningham had returned to Antarctica with Smith, Todd and
Gardner. Maclean had emigrated to Canada), Big Jim of the SMC
dropped in to the 'ville one night and while cooking his meal
explained how the Squirrels were going to take over the Glen by
defeating, in a fight, the remnants of the Creag Dhu. The wicked
grin on his large face hinted of a send-up not to be taken seriously.

Perhaps such rivalry has to exist, to play its part among the forces
which encourage men to advances and innovations. We should not
be too surprised that they occurred for our world was very male
dominated and conflicts between groups and even within them was
as common as friendship. It is interesting to note that while many of
the friendships have stood the test of time, changing shape as the
changing life cycle demands, the rivalries have disappeared. Time
changes everything. Ambitions are achieved or shelved as the body
weakens. Without ambition rivalry and conflict are no longer
required and with maturity xenophobia and drunkenness are
discarded for enlightenment and the careful maintenance of one's
ageing body. Things move on. New men, new challenges and no
doubt, new rivalries consign earlier conflicts to the footnotes of
history. As for those involved, it was but a passing moment in their
development. Bigger things have removed them from the narrow
confines and parochial conflicts of the 60s Glencoe. It all seems so
very long ago and now so very trivial when ranked beside the tragic
and untimely deaths of Cunningham and Bugs. The former
drowned while trying to rescue one of his students from the boiling
sea beneath the shores of Wales; the latter in a climbing accident in

Canada. Today everyone is friendly. In meetings the conflict recedes behind a rosy hue of nostalgia in which the struggles of yesterday are conspired against in silence lest they embarrass by reminding us of our lesser past.

66

BUTT OF LEWIS

GREAT
BERNERA
CALLANISH
STORNOWAY

LEWIS

MEALASBHAL

CLISHAM

HARRIS

RODEL

LOCHMADDY

PAIBLE

NORTH UIST

HOWMORE
HECLA
BEINN
MHOR

SOUTH UIST

Long Island Journey

BARRA

Long Island Journey

It was the mid-1970s; another lifetime.

Callaghan was grappling with a collapsing pound and watching his options shrink to the IMF begging-bowl. Italy seemed in much the same boat. The post-war economic miracle was floundering. I had just become married and mortgaged. The prospect of a full-time job loomed and with it superannuation and life insurance. The halcyon days of free-wheeling seemed to be over. Belatedly the illusions of the 1960s, of the endless highway, were fading. There was the need for a gesture, to use the time before the sands in the chamber ran out, to go where I'd never been, to the further reaches, the outer limits. For a controlled illusion.

That day you could have believed yourself headed for Tir nan Og, the Gael's land of eternal youth; sailing to Arcadia. I had cycled the short distance from Oban railway station on to the Caledonian MacBrayne boat in the harbour. Across the bay lay Kerrera bathed in sunshine. As the boat rounded it and headed for Mull, past Lismore with its Stevenson lighthouse, the Paps of Jura came into view. Having cleared the Sound of Mull we were in open water and Barra looked like a toy mountain in the distance. Rum and Eigg to the north, Coll and Tiree to the south and the whole hazily-drawn silhouette of the Long Island, were visible.

Formerly the whole archipelago as far south as Mingulay was inhabited but today Barra and neighbouring Vatersay are the farthest-south centres of population. Barra was in the possession of the MacNeills from the 11th century. In the harbour of Castlebay the outline of Kisimul castle seems to grow out of a small rocky islet. It was formerly a MacNeill stronghold whence Kisimul's galleys brought fire and rapine from Orkney to Ireland. Lack of pretension was never a MacNeill fault. In the past a herald announced from the battlements of Kisimul castle, 'MacNeil has dined. The kings,

princes, and others of the earth may now dine.' Today Kisimul may
be visited by boat from Castlebay but formerly it was not so easy.
Around 1700 the traveller Martin Martin was refused access in case
he betrayed its secrets to a foreign power; but then, he was a
Skyeman. At the turn of the century Castelbay was a great centre for
the herring industry; now most of the fish seen there are frozen into
fingers.

Barra is ideal cycling country. It is flat and I did the circuit of it in
an hour, allowing an evening crossing in a local motor boat, past the
famed and fabled Eriskay, where time permitted no stop, to land on
South Uist. As on Barra the road on Uist follows the flat coastal strip
but any ideas of an easy cycle were dispelled by a Hebridean head
wind so strong that dismounting and walking provided a faster pace.
It took all of three hours to cover the twelve miles to my destination.
This was the clachan of Howmore where the Gatliff Trust maintain
an open hostel in an old black house. In the mid-70s there were still
a few black houses in Howmore, without water and electricity. Mrs
MacSween, who had been 'at the peats', and who was the custodian,
told me the door was open and some people already there.

South Uist was formerly famed for its horses, which grazed the
machair on the west coast of the island. Today some crofters still
grow a mixture of oats and barley as animal fodder. Among the crops
grow poppies and corn marigolds. The sandy grassland of the
machair stretches for miles beside the Atlantic breakers. In spring
and summer it is a tapestry of clover, silverweed and milkwort. In
Howmore then you could have believed it would never be night
again. Walking behind the massive Kirk, by the shore after midnight,
it showed west like MacTaggart's seascape 'The Paps of Jura', that I
had gazed at in Kelvingrove Art Gallery. Blue sky, blue sea, blue
imagined mountains to the west, where lay Atlantis.

But it was eternal night for the blind rabbits, eyes burst and teeth
protruding; fodder for gulls and crows along the shore – the last
victims of myxomatosis. And night would have covered the wrecked
cars, fridges and cookers dumped by the locals in every available
hollow in the machair.

These blots on Arcadia did not trouble Lindy Lou from Palto

Alto, Ca., who was also staying at Howmore. She was one of those clean pretty and sexless American girls who would tour 'Yrp' and come back with their virginity intact and armpits clean. She seemed to spend all of her time washing (a time-consuming business from a cold stand-pipe) and writing up her diary. Over her shoulder once I caught her writing, 'I think the real me is coming out here'. She was pursued by an asthmatic Mancunian. His chest was bad, he said. He had been living in Howmore for six months, collecting his dole and breathing the Hebridean air which he felt was good for his chest. 'I'd like to see that chest of his', commented Mrs MacSween once. But as the Mancunian was as effete as Lindy was sexless, I was spared embarrassment at night, and he a possible asthmatic siezure.

Not all of South Uist is machair. The eastern half of the island is rough moorland; difficult walking country which rises to around 2,000 ft. Again luck was in. On the morning of a beautiful day I had a fine early start. The shape of the hills, the whaleback of Beinn Mhor and jagged peaks of Hecla and Ben Corodale, enticed me onto the moor. They looked so near. Then the peat road I followed stopped abruptly and I began to toil through peat-hags, tumbled rocks and deep heather.

Never, in Knoydart or elsewhere, have I experienced such rough terrain, such hard going, such slow progress. More than two hours elapsed before I began easing up the summit slope of Beinn Mhor, at last glimpsing the deserted east coast of the island to my left. Further off lay the north-west corner of Skye. On my right was a surprise; a stretch of clean cliff that looked climbable. In the Lakes, there would have been a guide-book. Lunch on top of Ben Corodale, twixt Hecla and Beinn Mhor, looking down on Usinish peninsula. Then on to Hecla itself over flat boiler-plates of rock.

The silence. Not a soul, not an animal, hardly a bird all day. I followed a long sloping ridge down from Hecla, which proved much easier than the ascent, cutting back across the peat-hags to my bike after a day longer and harder than on many mountains twice the size.

Next morning, while Lindy was at her ablutions and the Mancunian at his heavy breathing, Mrs MacSween burst in to tell us that the bread van at the road end had a box of kippers for sale. 'You'd better be at the hurrying if you'll be wanting one', she warned. And true enough as I pedalled away from the clachan the road was full of its inhabitants heading for the kippers. I stopped on my way out to talk to the local crofter who did the thatching, hard at work on Mrs MacSween's roof. No one else could do it now, he said, and it was becoming difficult to get the rushes.

Before heading north I took a short trip south to Ormiclate 'Castle', in ruins since it was burned after its owner, Alan of Clanranald was killed at Sheriff Muir in 1715. The tenant of the farm nearby showed me the forge in the castle, that he once used himself. There was little call for it now, with so few horses. In halting English he spoke of a Clanranald chief, who, shamed in front of his guests by a clansman eating a worm, shot him dead through a window. I wondered what Lindy would have made of that.

The road north goes past Loch Druidibeg (loch of the little starling), fringed with irises and afloat with water lilies, a home for mute swans and grey-lag geese. The last sight of South Uist was of locals at the sheep 'fank', shearing and dipping – like the peats, an activity still semi-communal in the Outer Isles.

A series of causeways connect South to North Uist. Between lies Benbecula. This seemed less scenically attractive to me and was heavily blighted by the military presence. Arcadia playing host to Armageddon. So I puffed on to North Uist, an island more moorland than machair and more water than moorland. The rain began to fall and I sheltered for a while, and lunched, in a chambered cairn. But it was a cold lodgings and again in the rain I moved on to the Teampull na Trionaid, a ruined outpost of Christianity in times when the Norsemen raided. Duns Scotus, the medieval philosopher, whose followers were dubbed 'Dunses', is said to have studied here. The French are Cartesians, the Germans Hegelians, the Scots, Dunses. This thought gave little comfort in the howling wind and now lashing rain as the miles towards Paible were covered. I was becoming desperate for shelter.

A drenched billboard advertised the Paible Highland Games and looking into the adjacent field I saw the tents. Frozen children

huddled in the refreshment tent where I took shelter. Out back the
young blades drank their whisky in the Hebridean storm. A piping
competition was taking place in the lee of a tent, with the judges
holding down their hats, and the notes disappearing in the wind.
The locals did not feel that they had much chance against the men
from South Uist, outstanding in that area since the days of
Clanranald. The storm cleared and I left, with the contest not over
but neither in doubt.

I found a warm caravan to hire in Lochmaddy, dried out, and next
day crossed with 'Cal-Mac' to Tarbet, Harris. Once more the
weather had improved and at low tide the sea between the two
islands looked like a continuous beach glistening in the sunlight.
Harris is probably the loveliest of the Hebrides; to find beaches such
as exist here, Bermuda or the Seychelles would have to be visited.
But none of these could offer the isolation of the Harris beaches, or
the views north to its mountains. The beaches are on the west while
the east coast is rocky and indented.

Economic success has always been elusive in the Outer Isles with
limited tourism (due to distance) and no natural resources.
Emigration continues to be the answer and many are retired after a
lifetime of work elsewhere. Others survive by occupying a variety of
seasonal part-time jobs. Harris has many testimonies to economic
failure. At Leverburgh are the relics of Lord Leverhume's attempts
to establish a fishing station after the First World War. And at
Bunavoneadar are the ruins, including a fine chimney-stack, of a
whaling station once used by the Norwegians.

The traditional poverty of the Outer Isles can be seen in the lack
of many substantial stone-built historical monuments, such as exist
for example in the richer Orkneys. Nevertheless Harris boasts the
jewel of the Outer Hebrides, an Iona in miniature – the Church of
St. Clement's at Rodel. This contains many fine carved Macleod
tombs including that of Alexander Macleod from 1528. In the
graveyard is buried Donald Macleod who took part in the '45
Rebellion when over 50 and whose greater achievement is also
recorded on his tombstone – 'In his 75th year he married his third

wife, by whom he had nine children and died in his 90th year.' On the Kirk wall 'stands' a figure with enormous, but damaged, phallus. The local laird's wife had ordered her gamekeeper to blast the offending instrument off the church despite it being a medieval addition to the structure. Many symbols are there for those who seek them. Sitting at Rodel harbour watching the gannets plunge I felt uplifted by my visit to holy ground.

And uplifted too by my visit to the local pub, the Rodel Hotel. This was built in the late 18th century as were the harbour works. It survives little changed from the aquatint made of it by William Daniell in the early 19th century. The entrance hall is still flagged and a huge rough dresser bore a set of crockery that looked as if it had been shipped in with the flags. An old grandfather-clock ticked heavily as I waited. A long time.

But the hotel was closed and I needs go next door to the jerry-built annexe for my meat and drink. But this was no loss for I met a garrulous group of locals there.

"Whateffer are you wanting to be cycling for? You can get the postbus now!"

"What's your hurry? If you don't get to Stornoway today, you'll get there tomorrow. And they're all Lewismen there, nothing but ministers!"

"A lot of good men came from Aberdeen but a lot of better men came out of it!"

"You liff in Klasgow now? There's no city in the world I luff better than Klasgow. I was a policeman there for thirty years..."

"Your wife is from Skye then? Well, that's not so bad."

It was late when I departed the pub.

Next day I took the road from Tarbet to the Lews. This goes over the shoulder of The Clisham; the highest mountain in the Outer Isles, a full 600 ft higher than Beinn Mhor. But it gave a much easier ascent than Beinn Mhor. Even without a path the climb from where I left the bike was easy, the ground firm and less rugged, reaching the summit by a narrowing ridge. From thence I could see Loch Seaforth to the east and away to the west the fantastic outline of

Hirta. The trackless country to the north, by Loch Langabhat, was a patchwork of loch and moor; a boat would be more useful there than a bike, I thought.

That evening I made Stornoway and wandered round the harbour where the regulations were in English, Gaelic and Russian. Locals who still fish sell their catches to the Klondykers, mainly East European, who buy up the whole catch.

From Stornoway to the Butt of Lewis is uniformly peat bog and there has been talk of using local peat to fire a power station, as in Eire, so rich is the supply. The Butt itself is the scene of fantastic cliffs rich in bird life, including the 'Guga', which the Lewis men attest to be a gastronomic delicacy and which is sent to exiles every year at Christmas.

From the Butt the road goes south through populated crofting townships and passes some dramatic historical remains. At Carloway is possibly the best-preserved broch outside of Shetland, with double wall, entrance and internal stair, as well as part of the corbel still intact. Some of the nearby sheep pens, however, seem to have been constructed from the broch in less conservation-conscious days. The mysterious Broch-builders were superseded by the Norsemen, who held the Isles for centuries till 1263 and whose tongue has left its mark on the place names of the Hebrides, though surprisingly little on the spoken Gaelic. The Norsemen also built several of their simple click-mills in Lewis. These were still in use in the last century; one is at Barvas.

The only accommodation I could find that night was in the house of what must have been the earliest white settlers in this part of Lewis. Let us call them Basil and Thelma. They had retired early and were fleeing what they saw as 'Britain going to the dogs': inflation, strikes, comprehensive education. Blinkered and bitter they thought they had found a refuge. Basil fulminated against striking railwaymen who were holding up his DIY materials. Thelma denounced the lazy and untrustworthy locals, for whom she had a racist disdain matching his hatred of the lower classes. Basil put on a Richard Clayderman record. There was no needle and the arm screamed across the disk. In the morning Thelma made porridge with condensed milk; I had to pour it down the toilet. As I left, she checked 'to see that I'd left nothing' (that I had stolen nothing). A defender of railwaymen and comprehensive education was capable of anything.

The main monument of the Outer Isles is the Stonehenge of the North, the standing-stones at Callanish. Formerly thought to be Christian in origin because of their cruciform shape, they are in fact from a much earlier date though experts still dispute their function, whether religious, astronomical or both. This expert saw them as a place for a welcome rest from pedalling and the sure-fire location of a fortifying tea shop, to kill the taste of the porridge.

On from Callanish the ground becomes hillier in the direction of Uig. Here in the west of Lewis one looks south to a horizon blocked by the mountains of Harris. The island of Great Bernera was my target, to check if any remains were left of the airidhs used by my mother-in-law between the wars. Seton-Gordon remarked in 1935, in his *Highways and Byways in the West Highlands*, of the airidhs (summer shielings),

> Lewis...is the only district of the highlands and islands where the summer shieling still lives. In the small thatched shielings they remain until the end of the summer (with) their cattle, and...allow the grass of the townships' grazing to grow a crop sufficient for the winter feed.

But even in Lewis this practice did not survive the war. Nowadays the airidhs are as likely to be used as drinking bothans as anything. But I did find my airidh. It was roofless and without the furniture and lath that its tiny proportions held half a century ago.

The airidh is not used. There are no cattle now and the milk comes from Stornoway as does the rest of the food. Indeed there is no agriculture on the island, the cultivated land reverted to bracken and moor, the inhabitants mostly pensioners. The tidal lobster-pot, its wall breached, is a fine form for monochrome photography but no one comes to collect the crustaceans which escape through the gaps at low tide. An economy ruined, marginalised as surely as the economy of lowland Scotland was now being destroyed in the

Airidh, Lewis

economic crisis laying waste its traditional industries. The Lowland
Clearances, temporarily left behind. Out of sight, out of mind.

And I found out two old relatives by marriage who told tales of the
summer nights in the airidhs between the wars, when the village lads
came out to see the lasses tending the cattle and there was singing
and laughing. And of how my mother-in-law was admired by the
local lads, since, a Glasgow Highlander on holiday, she could speak
proper English as well as the Gaelic. And they told me of the men of
Bernera who fought eviction and marched to Stornoway in 1874 to
confront their land-owner. The old warm hatred of the exploiting
classes still burned in the telling. And told old folk tales, such as that
of the fugitive, reputed a cannibal, Mac an t-Sronach who lived in
the Uig hills and who was used to control generations of children.

'Mac an t-Sronach will get you!' Next day they showed me their future resting places among their forebears in the island graveyard. They are there now.

> It is a grey world, sea and sky
> Are colourless as the grey stones...
> Into the cemetery where on an unfenced sandhill
> The grey memorial stones of the island
> Have no distinction from the country.
> (MacDiarmid *Island Funeral*.)

The hills of Uig had not changed much since Mac an t-Sronach roamed them a century and a half ago. Trackless I found them, even beyond those of South Uist. Behind me lay Uig sands, to my right was Canada, as I stepped onto the moor leading towards Mealasbhal the highest point in Lewis. The peat road ended after a mile and the rutted peat-hags, waist-deep in vegetation, began. I passed several ruined airidhs by Loch Mor na Clibhe before thankfully pulling out of the heather and peat to the boulder-strewn slopes of Mealasbhal. From the top Hirta was visible but nearer to hand Scarp and Sron Ulladale in the Harris hills were slowly vanishing in a haze. The weather turned as I toiled on towards Cracabhal. I had fondly imagined doing the whole Uig horseshoe in a day but my illusions vanished as the mist thickened and the wind whipped at my face. So I descended to Loch Roanasgail and struggled back to my starting point, brought to earth and defeated by the terrain and weather. My admiration for Mac an t-Sronach, surviving here seven years, was unbounded.

The Long Island works its magic on many who visit it. Many see the mermaids, the silkies, swimming with the seals; and hear the mermaids sing. But unlike Prufock, feel they sing for them. Here is one who felt thus,

Over the horizon is the Land of the Ever-Young, a land whose treasures are a sense of awe and wonder, physical and mental renewal and spiritual growth; a land where, for the Argonauts who quest after it, is to be found the Golden Fleece. (*Argonauts of the Western Isles* Lloyd Jones)

There is no Golden Fleece; for Basil, or Thelma, or Lindy Lou – or
for you. What you run away to reflects all that you run away from.
But you can have small victories provided you practise the realpolitik
of ambition; you can find your airidh. A shelter from the storm. As
Mac an t-Sronach said on the gallows,

> A mhointich riabhaich Leodhais:
> Agus fhad's a ghleidh mis' thus'
> Ghleidh thusa mis'
>
> O brown moors of Lewis,
> as long as I kept to you,
> you preserved me.

Hebrides Log

STORR ROCK
X

RONA

ISLE

HALLAIG

PORTREE

RAASAY

LOCH
BRACADALE

STRUAN

OF

SKYE

THE CUILLIN

BLAVEN

JOHN
NORMAN
COLLIE
1859-1942

LOCH
SCAVAIG

LOCH
SLAPIN

SLEAT

BARRISDALE
BAY

LADHAR
BHEINN

LUINNE
BHEINN

KNOYDART

INVERIE

MEALL BUIDHE

RUM

Sea of
the
Hebrides

The Log from the Sea of the Hebrides

Acairseid Mhor, Rona.

Leaning on the harbour rails I watched the 'Callisto', a thirty foot Bermudan sloop, bobbing at anchor. Drizzle fell and heavy clouds scudded towards Raasay. Like the clouds, thoughts moved fleeting and oppressive and I pondered why I was at Portree waiting for the boat's owner. To use the yacht as a base to do a few more Munros difficult of access? Or was it something engendered by the relentless approach of the shadow line of forty, a Tilmanesque leap, to 'sail beyond the sunset...until I die' (Tennyson). The rain eased off and a dinghy approached shore from the boat before the question was answered.

Tim, the boat's owner, rowed me out to the 'Callisto' and asked if I'd done any sailing before. "My nautical experience consists of a couple of trips 'Doon the Watter' in the Waverley paddle-steamer. But I'd a great grandfather who invented a fishing boat, the 'Zulu' a hundred years ago. So maybe it's in the blood." He gave me a quizzical look.

But by 10 o'clock, anchored at Acairseid Mhor (the Big Anchorage) on Rona my doubts, if not his, had vanished. Clearly there wasn't much to sailing after all. We'd motored out of Portree harbour and then got the sails up. I even took a turn at the tiller. A brief sail across the Sound of Raasay showed the Trotternish Ridge and the Old Man of Storr etched by the setting sun, before we glided into the anchorage, wooded round the shore.

Over the evening meal and a few rounds of the local vintage (Talisker), we discussed what to do with the time available. The other two on board, Kevin and Donnie, were willing to fall in with my plans to sail to Knoydart and spend a douple of days there, before moving on to Coruisk in Skye to tackle Blaven. We bedded early, to rise early and catch the tide.

Barrisdale Bay, Knoydart.

The sleeping quarters were bunks; not a hammock in sight. But I slept badly due to the unaccustomed motion of the boat. After breakfast we went ashore to examine the ruined house facing us. It gave evidence of having been used as a bothy. There were three packets of Ruskoline on the table; maybe someone had high expectations of the fishing? The island is now untenanted but for the sheep and a Navy submarine-tracking station at the north end. Rona is also a candidate for the dumping of nuclear waste. Military birds of prey flew down the Sound at supersonic speeds, scattering the herons from their roostings. But the dolphins guided us safely through between Rona and Raasay while the black whales of war basked in the sun towards Applecross.

As we sailed into the choppier waters of the Inner Sound, Kevin pointed out Hallaig, birthplace of Sorley Maclean, on Raasay's now deserted east coast. Maclean's, *Hallaig* speaks of the clearances in Raasay;

> The window is nailed and boarded
> through which I saw the West
> and my love is at the Burn of Hallaig
> a birch tree...
>
> ...I will go down to Hallaig
> to the Sabbath of the dead
> which the people are frequenting
> every single generation gone.

There is new life on Raasay; incomers, outdoor pursuits centres.

Unusual views of the Cuillin came and went in the shifting cloud. An invitation to camera work. Tim relieved me of my fumbling attempts at the tiller and set the others to man the sails, while I shot at Pinnacle Ridge and Clach Glas from angles unaccustomed on land. We speeded up, aiming to pass the narrows at Kyleakin before midday, after which the tide would be against us. Relegated to the function of cabin boy I made tea for the crew and noticed how the boat picked up speed with the tide as we sped past the Crowlin Islands. Passing through the narrows I hoped our trip would be more successful than that of the man who gave them their name: Hacon, defeated at the Battle of Largs after passing through the Kyles.

Rounding the point towards Kylerhea it became markedly choppier and windier. This did not deter a party out in a small boat, tending the lights on isolated rocks and skerries. We had to beat through the narrows; hard work on the tiller for the paying guest and harder for those manning the sails. I wondered how the poor beasts going to the cattle trysts managed to swim the narrows in bygone days, given the tide race.

Tacking into Loch Hourn the cloud lifted a little, but not enough to destroy the illusion of being in a fjord, steep sides rising to vanish in the mist. By the time we dropped anchor just west of Barrisdale Bay we had been sailing for 10 hours and covered about thirty-five miles. Sailing at walking pace. We retired, hoping the mist would lift next day for Ladhar Bheinn.

Upper Loch Hourn.

We moved here in the evening, as last night's anchorage was too exposed to westerly winds predicted by the weather forecast. That litany of romantic names at last meant something to me. Dogger, Malin, Hebrides...Near-hurricane gales were punishing the south of England. "Serves them right for voting Tory," commented Kevin who hails from that airt, but likes to think himself a Skyeman now. He certainly had the open, unaffected friendliness of the Skyeman. After taking depth soundings, Tim finally hitched to a mooring on a fish farm belonging to one of the ex-members of a famous pop group. The splash of the leaping fish was the only noise to break the silence, bar the faint cries from the heronry further up the loch. And the unwanted visit from two white settlers from their holiday home, expressing regret that the Army didn't get the Knoydart estate. We were too polite but silence eventually drove them away.

On the way up the loch we passed a wild goat on an island off Barrisdale. He had probably swum there and seemed at a loss how to get off, watching us hopefully as we passed within a few feet of him.

We had rowed ashore in the morning, and attacked Ladhar

Bheinn 'diretissima'; a fair pech, as all agreed. Uneventfully the summit cairn was reached in cold mist but on beginning to tackle the circuit of the hill it cleared to give views of Skye and Torridon. Apart from the steep slabby descent of Stob a' Chearcaill, the hill is of no technical difficulty. It gives less of a ridge walk than expected from below, since it slopes off gently southwards. A pleasant and rather leisurely day, and back to the boat after six hours out.

Tomorrow Tim will sail single-handed round to Inverie while the rest of us cross Knoydart to meet up with him. Hopefully tonight I'll get another sleep of the dead.

Inverie, Knoydart.

The day dawned rosy and bright and till midday looked set for a scorcher. At 9.00 Tim disembarked us at Barrisdale and we ambled past the bothy. It looked much gentrified since I was last there and people moved around behind the windows. We took a fine stalkers' path up through birch woods in the sunlight, up the glen towards Luinne Bheinn. But by the time we gained the col looking down towards the tantalising sand-fringed Lochan nam Breac it had closed in. We ascended the wide broken ridge to the summit in shifting mist. At the top it cleared to show Meall Bhuide, our next objective, at what seemed a fair distance and a long descent and re-ascent away. But we dropped to the bealach in twenty minutes. Though the going was hard, as befits the 'Rough Bounds', it was dry. Thus we soon reached the top of Meal Buidhe in a cool wind – four and a half hours out from Barrisdale. Below us we could see the descent to Inverie and the sails of the 'Callisto' heading thither. The delight of not having to retrace our steps sunk in. We stopped to rest and eat.

Donnie and Kevin lay back with a 'roll up' after the meal. Both were very fit from working in the forestry. Like Tim, who hails from Cumbria, their economic existence as incomers is varied and precarious; forestry, fishing and odd-jobbing. The locals distinguish between working incomers, and the red-necked white settler breed, Kevin stated.

"But you're still never really accepted," said Donnie.

After many years on Skye he is off to try his luck in the South Seas for a couple of years.

On the descent fatigue set in and I dropped behind the others. I was too tired to leave the path and piss on Lord Brocket's monument on the outskirts of Inverie. Brocket was the laird who would not let the locals walk in front of Inverie House; they spoiled the view. He owned the estate pre-war and entertained prominent Nazis there, visiting the Führer himself in Germany. After the war his tenants, returned from active service, seized untilled land behind Inverie and began to cultivate it. The fascist laird got the courts to evict the anti-fascist servicemen, most of whom left, and Inverie went into terminal decline. The ballad *The Men of Knoydart*, by Hamish Henderson, describes the affair. Fishgut Mac used to sing this with great gusto. In reply to Brocket's threats,

> You Highland swine, these hills are mine!
> This is all Lord Brocket's land.

Mac would give back

> O we are all ex-servicemen
> We fought against the Hun
> We can tell our enemies by now,
> And Brocket you are one!

But the raiders were evicted, nonetheless.

At this point there was a consolation. Proving, as the Bible says, 'He who is last, will be first'. I reached the pier at Inverie to await Kevin and Donnie, after being given a lift by a rickety Land-rover. The occupants had been brought in to work at the House, now a huntin', shootin', fishin' establishment for paying guests. Inverie had also changed since my visit in '82. The old estate club is now a pub and there is even a tea shop. Many of the empty houses have been spruced up to greet the influx of population. Tourism rather than agriculture is seen as the economic salvation of Knoydart. At night the pub was jammed with bothiers, tourists and yachtsmen. There was not a local in sight. Lord Brocket had won after all.

We'd hit the town, dragging the dinghy up the beach, to celebrate Donnie's birthday. He'd reached the Big Four-O before me. We got pretty well-oiled, leaving the pub at midnight to row back to the boat. In the black night we moved slowly, phosphorescence gleaming on the water falling from the oars. Blacker against the black sky were the mountains of Knoydart.

In the boat the conversation turned, as it will with men of a certain age in certain places, to the meaning of life. The times, the philistine, heartless times and rule by reptiles, were cursed. As was our following generation, of yuppies or junkies, hopeless to prevail against them. We tacked in and out of blind alleys and mazes of private solutions. Near 2 o'clock general exhaustion set in and drove all to bed.

In the morning Donnie was convinced he'd solved the riddle of existence, but forgotten the answer while he slept. The rest of us couldn't remember either.

Loch Slapin.
Awoke to a beautiful morning and for the first and only time managed some sun-bathing as we ate breakfast on deck. Sgurr na Ciche looked particularly dramatic in the morning haze at the head of Loch Nevis. But is was chilly by the time we lifted anchor. We motored to Mallaig, racing the Inverie ferry, but lost by quite a bit despite a head start. At Mallaig Kevin jumped ship to go camping with wife and children and the depleted crew headed off towards the Point of Sleat and the far Cuillin. Quite a long sail this, and slow; beating against the wind as Knoydart disappeared into the mist and rain behind us. But ahead Rum and Eigg delighted, like cardboard cut-outs on the Minch.

Tacking into Loch Slapin, it calmed. Views emerged that quickened the pulse and had hands reaching for cameras. Clach Glas was like a huge battlement, the Inaccessible Pinnacle an impregnable sanctuary proof in brief illusion. The anchor was dropped late and darkness forced us below decks to eat and sleep.

Loch Bracadale, Skye.
Today the idea was for Tim to sail our aquatic taxi to Coruisk, or precisely, to Loch Scavaig; 'the most dramatic anchorage in Europe' according to the Clyde Cruising Club publication I flicked through.

We, meanwhile, would traverse Blaven and come round to Coruisk by Camasunary. Our row ashore stirred the herons fishing at the mouth of the Kilmarie burn. We ascended, Donnie and I, by an indistinct path to Coir'an Uaigneis where we stopped for refreshment at a lovely high lochan. But again it misted over as we ascended the scree between Blaven and Clach Glas, leaving the rest of the Cuillin only briefly and fragmentarily clear from the summit. I looked down the scree shoot on which I'd destroyed my first pair of boots twenty years ago. Then, mapless, I'd missed the highest top of Blaven. A modest achievement, a small victory, to be there now.

The bothy at Camasunary came into view on descending the easy south ridge of Blaven, route of its first ascent by the poet Swinburne. And beyond that we saw the 'Callisto' heading for Coruisk. At Camasunary, where I had spent the wettest two days of my life that Easter, there was no one to offer us a brew. A huge Pinnacle Ridge of rubbish had been assembled on the beach, awaiting removal; the plastic flotsam and jetsam of the modern fishing industry.

On now, skirting the base of Sgurr na Stri. Donnie asked me if my expectations of the week had been realised. No rural Eden had been sought or found. But I had done four hills in the dogged pursuit of the useless tally. By the actual calculus I now used, not a defeat. So I said yes.

On rounding the headland from Camasunary the Cuillin came into view, generous as ever with the actuality of the dramatic. In mixed sun and rain the boiler-plate slabs of the Dubhs glistened, while on the left the leaning summit of Gars-bheinn looked like Tatlin's monument to the Third International. Amidst all this the Bad Step was an anti-climax, not hard enough to be graded easy. In fact we thought we had missed it. At Scavaig the JMCS hut was boarded and empty. There was just time to snap the 'Callisto' at her moorings before being rowed out to her in a heavy shower.

We had intended to moor there but the forecast for the next day was bad. Tim thus favoured a run to Bracadale and shelter in the evening, avoiding the anticipated Force eight winds next day. Without eating we set sail past tidal rocks rolling with fat seals at the Scavaig outlet and stopped below Gars-bheinn to fish. Donnie

Loch Scavaig

pulled out five mackerel on his first attempt but my effort to add to the tally proved fruitless. As we moved along the deserted shore below the Cuillin we were rewarded with perspectives unattainable from the land. We picked out the Thearlaich-Dubh Gap, and White Slab on Coir'a' Ghrunnda readily. Talk turned to climbing and ideas of the perfect day. "A nice long V-Diff," smiled Tim and I agreed. I'd readily have swopped something much harder for what followed.

The Cuillin had tempted me below for my camera. Under deck the first attack of nausea came on, from loss of a frame of reference.

"Keep your eyes on the horizon, it helps," suggested Tim. We headed out on a long tack towards Rum, then back to Loch Eynort, out again towards Canna before heading back to Talisker Bay, beating against the unfavourable wind. Although it was 'only' Force seven it was too much for me. The boat listed heavily, at times the water seemed vertically below me. I suffered, hanging on to the mast. But by fixing on the horizon and muttering nursery rhymes to myself I took my mind off my misery and avoided being sick. At one point I nearly wept in despair; we seemed to be headed straight for South Uist. Surely there was no need for this?

Humpty Dumpty sat on a wall
Humpty Dumpty had a great fall...

The calmer, but misty waters of Loch Bracadale. Macleod's Maidens and Tables formed a screen print in variegated tones of black and grey that managed to impress over physical abjection. Skye – the inexhaustible, the outlasting.

Once the boat was at anchor a rapid recovery allowed me to join in finishing off the Talisker and picking the flesh from the bones of the mackerel. Tim smiled at my recovery, adding, "I don't think we'll make a sailor out of you."

I didn't accept Tim's verdict and tried again. The next year a brief weekend trip, in idyllic weather, fostered my illusions. We motored on a glass sea to North Uist, heading for a blood red sun on the horizon. We had a following wind next day to Rodel in Harris and watched the gannets diving in the spring sunshine by the pier. And rising early we beat the worst of an approaching storm to stroll on the coral beach at Dunvegan, after sleeping at anchor while the storm passed over us there. So the following year again would be reserved for Rum and a traverse of its Cuillin with Jack and Alec.

The best summer of the decade broke as we arrived; for three days force eight and nine winds blew and the rain lashed down. In intervals between the fronts we fished, strolled on coastal islands, motored round headlands, pleitered. Halfway through the week we were still in Bracadale. After a day when we could not even put the dinghy on water and land, it appeared to lift. We decided to make a run for Canna's sheltered harbour whence, if it settled fair, we might be able to make Rum. I'd been reading Gunn's *Off In A Boat*, where he describes being imprisoned in Bracadale for nearly two weeks. I wasn't prepared to suffer that.

We made slow progress to Bracadale Head. Slower when we rounded it in the teeth of the gale and in the narrow jaw of the running Hebridean tide. Here the whole Minch is funnelled into the fourteen miles between Skye and Uist. The boat strained through the waves and at once I was floored with sea-sickness. Tim gave me tablets and sent me below where I lay on the floor, shivering and curled into a sleeping bag, the epitome of misery. "We'll make it if it doesn't get any worse," I heard our captain say.

It was ten hours before anyone spoke to me, ten hours till I could ask what had happened. I knew it was getting worse. I was being rolled violently from side to side, try and wedge myself in as I would. Soon the boat was keeling so much that all its contents were thrown loose; books, pans, clothes were flying everywhere at each lurch. The fold-away table worked loose and struck me on the head. In the moments before the boat lurched back I could hear the sea, its hiss and slap. Now and again through the side windows I could see booted feet moving past.

Drugged, I dozed. Until the thumps started. A great cacophony of blows and bangs which seemed to be coming from below me. Yes, the impact was definitely coming from underneath me. At each one I was hurled in the air and then left to fall back to the floor. There was no sky when I turned my head to the windows now, only sea. The pan I had retched into had long since spilled its contents onto the floor. I was aware that if an emergency occurred, I could not raise myself from the ground.

I was as glad as hell I was not on deck and blanked my mind against what might be hapening as again the boat was lifted from the water, then hurled back into it. For so it seemed to me.

Calmness. Suddenly the tempest ceased; everything was quiet.

Tim appeared in the cabin entry and asked how I was.

"Are we there?" I asked in return.

"We're going back," was all he said, closing the hatch.

With the tide running for us and the wind behind us we made six knots on the way back – without any sail. This had been torn in the storm and when the mast had threatened to snap, Tim ordered a turn-around. We, they, had got to within a mile of Canna harbour, trying to sneak in by crawling along the north coast. Near enough to see the fern fronds on the shore. It had been Force eleven.

Though they were sodden to the skin, frozen to the marrow and weak with hunger, I could not rise to help them. And they had not shared my fear; they had been too busy. But what they had done that day I could not share or even comprehend, divorced from their experience below deck.

"They were great," Tim simply said.

Relief at being below decks gave way to a sneaking envy.

Bracadale.

This morning Skye mist blotted out everything on the foreshore. Tim, Donnie and I took a trip to the Church at Struan and after hacking our way through damp bracken found the graves of Collie and Mackenzie. Modest memorials, unattended. Their real memorials are the peaks which bear their names in the Cuillin. The chemist and the crofter, commemorated by the gabbro obelisks of Sgurr Thormaid and Sgurr Mhic Choinnich.

Collie came to Skye and found what he sought: an inexhaustible source of joy in the still largely virgin Cuillin and a lifelong friend in Britain's first professional mountain guide. So deep and lasting was their friendship that Collie wished his bones to rest beside those of the man from Sconser, whom he described as follows,

> ....a most loveable, charming and delightful companion...As a companion on a long summer day he was perfect...Those who knew him will remember him as a perfect gentleman, one who never offended by word or deed. (SMC Journal, Vol 20).

Collie lived out his last years at Sligachan and made Struan his final resting place. 'Home from the sea', we knew that our search today could only have more modest objectives, not that for a resting place. There was no waiting rural Utopia, free from the pressures that drove us to seek it; everywhere cultural entropy reproduced what we left behind.

Outward Bound

These are the days of endless summer
These are the days the time is now.
These are the days now that we must savour
And enjoy them while we can
These are the days that will last forever
You've got to hold them to your heart.
(Van Morrison).

These are the days of endless summer. I stretch my legs as the plane lifts itself over Arran. I look down through the little window. Grey mountains set in green, afloat on a dazzling blue sea. It could be any millionaire's paradise. Last weekend it belonged to Higgins and me as we climbed that most exquisite piece of rock, the South Ridge of Cir Mhor. This weekend I am bound for America to work for Outward Bound in Colorado.

Flying, even for someone as new to it as I am, is such a boring activity. Six hours over the top of the world. Underneath, the disembodied voice of the pilot tells us, there is Greenland and soon Baffin Island. But they are covered by cloud. Landing is an exciting activity. We bump around for what seems like hours in thick mists, turning this way, then that, until I am sure that the cool pilot cannot possibly know where we are. In my ignorance, anxiety is contained by a certainty that everything must be alright. Across the aisle two women hold hands and cry softly into white handkerchiefs. Perhaps I should reappraise my certainties. Then without warning, when we seem indecently close to it, the ground springs from the mists. There are big pick-up trucks near the runway. I know I am in America.

I stand in the rain looking at the big cars swishing softly through puddles. They have rain and puddles in New York! It seems so quiet! Does culture shock mean that one is startled by the banal while losing the power of one's ears? My mind seems fixated by these strange thoughts. I cannot move. But there is a policeman in dark-blue double-breasted jacket, carrying a long stick. I have heard the only way to approach a New York policeman is with a ten dollar bill in one's hand. If you ask them the direction they snort, "Buy yourself a map buddy." But I panic and ask him anyway. He does not club me to the ground but waves his stick vaguely in the direction of a bus.

The bus is driven by a young Marlon Brando in a white tee-shirt. He grudgingly gives me change for the ticket machine and agrees to let me know when we reach the subway terminus.

It is still raining. I am dressed in a red jacket. I have a large pack on my back, attached to which is a short ice axe. I am walking down a street to a subway, which is above the street carried on one of those bridges seen so many times in the cinema. There are only black faces, and I am prejudiced enough to think I can be attacked at any time. Instead the youths on the corners make good-humoured jokes about Santa Claus coming early.

At the Port Authority on 42nd Street, I pick my way through the junkies, the dealers, the drag queens and rhinestone cowboys to find a bus which leaves for Denver in half an hour. Aboard and moving, I admit to myself that I am not one of nature's travellers. I feel as though I have escaped from hell.

By the time we reach the New Jersey turnpike I relax a little. It is dark, and by the side of the road every few miles, there are large screens on which there are moving pictures. It takes me a minute to work out what they are. Drive-in Movies! I subside in my seat thinking tunelessly about Simon and Garfunkel and 'We're all off to search for America'. Or am I on the road with Kerouac? Romantics are often confused.

Through the night and through West Virginia, we skirt round the north end of the Appalachians stopping every two hours or so at road-side diners. There are grey-lined faces under the neon, for only the old and poor in America travel by bus. By daybreak we have left the Blue Ridge Mountains behind. It is on to St. Louis, Missouri and Kansas City and beyond, the great fertile American plains. I lift my head from my book every so often and gaze out through the window. We do not appear to have moved. Surely it was the same flat vista of cereals which was there before. Yet there is movement, measured by the passing of small towns each one identical to the last: Junction City, Abilene, Salina and on into the Smokey Hills – Russel, Hays and Ellis, a dusty main street consisting of single storey buildings – a bar, a store, some place selling agricultural machinery. A few dusty pick-up trucks are parked at the sidewalk but there are almost no people to be seen. A railroad stop above which towers the grain silo. The only thing that changes is the light! No matter at which time of day entry is made, the town is bathed in a light alien to Northern Europeans. At midday, under a high sun it is eye-itching white, its shadows short and black. In the evening, its rays hung on dust, the sun sets in burning orange grains down the centre of the westward highway on which we journey.

Each town gives up its passengers: the odd fat man among the majority of women. Small old ladies whose blue-rinsed hair and rhinestone-bedecked spectacles seem mandatory. There is the occasional young woman, her hair long and lank, her face pale. The marks of poverty. They move from one small town to another, to attend to their mysterious business.

After a while I become aware of something strange. The bus is often full yet no one sits beside me unless every other seat is taken. People even choose to sit beside the toilet at the rear rather than sit beside me. Given how peculiar Americans are about toilets – they will not admit what goes on in them and call them "rest rooms"; they carry paper covers to put on the seats so that their skin will not feel the warmth of their predecessor's – I begin to feel very foreign and isolated. I have cut my hair, bathed meticulously at every opportunity and wear conservative clothes, yet so obviously foreign must I appear that these innately conservative people steer well clear of me. I might be a Russian spy counting the grain silos for Moscow.

Then, when all the seats except the one beside me are filled, from one of these dull towns emerges an exotic creature. He is tall, black and incredibly beautiful in a threatening kind of way. The impact is

heightened by his immaculate uniform, for he wears the blue jacket
and white cap of the US Marines. He is encrusted with honours
culled no doubt from the deadly imbroglio of Vietnam. Here is my
opportunity, my guide to the very soul of small-town America and its
current consuming passion – the defence of its freedom in South-
east Asia. I must choose my words carefully and start with the topic
that never fails back home – the weather. "It's warm, isn't it?" He
turns and looks at me in the same way he would regard an
ambushing Vietcong, his glance as withering as 'agent orange'. Thus
I am destined to count the silos and ride my lonely way to Denver.

Still there is time to think why I have come here. I have no clear
idea regarding the use of mountains as a form of education. My own
philosophy of my involvement with the hills was simple enough. I
enjoy it. I enjoy the sense of exploration and discovery of beautiful
yet difficult places. I enjoy the feelings of achievement defined
according to one's ability, fitness and inclination. And perhaps most
of all I enjoy the bizarrely anarchic free spirits of the people I meet. I
have come to Outward Bound this summer to discover that its
philosophy was strangely at odds with this.

Kurt Hahn, the man who gave the world Outward Bound did so
because he thought the youth of peacetime required the 'moral
equivalent of war'. I find this a bizarre concept. Presumably he felt
that war brings out the best in people – reveals hidden qualities of
character and makes people work together with a will. The
difficulties and discomfort in going to the mountains, it is thought,
will produce the same results. He seemed to have forgotten about
the massacres of the innocents. Perhaps he believed that only the
other – evil – side carried them out. Climbers, as W.H. Murray
pointed out, are no better than other men, and although there are no
massacres in the 'moral equivalent of war', we would be foolish to
imagine that climbing eradicates the baser side of man's tempera-
ment. Consequently among even leading exponents one will
discover envy, greed, lust, bullying and ridicule for the efforts of
others.

Neither does climbing necessarily bring happiness or a release
from the pressures of everyday life. On the contrary, some like

Perrin when admitting 'the times when I have been best at climbing
have been the least happy times of my life', condemn an obsessive
interest in climbing as a trap of egocentricity and restraint which
denies the climber the 'creative act of living'.

My first group are at war with themselves and the mountains.
There is fear. Everyone fears the big mountains and big rivers; fear
of the unknown, fear of failure, the fear of death. Junkies drying out,
trust-fund kids cut off from their life-support systems fear the huge
voids, the darkness of the forests and the long Colorado nights.
There are no light switches and they are the lost children of the
cities.

The blacks and the whites fear each other. I have racial
confrontation on my hands. They are almost like caricatures. One
white boy from South Carolina is pious and full of religion; his
assumed superiority grates on the blacks. The other white boy from
Tenessee is a real 'cracker' who makes no effort to hide his disdain
for the blacks. He says of my efforts to bring peace "Ya all don know
how to handle them black boys." He hints at sterner methods than
my attempts to reason with everybody. He wants to kill 'gooks' in
Vietnam. I do not know how to handle him without being rude. The
black guys arrive with tennis rackets and fishing rods. What have
they been told about this course? One is slim, sharp-witted and
street-wise – a leader. The other is big, lazy and slow-witted. From
the first day he hates the course, the mountains and the people. He
spends his days kicking rocks and muttering incantations to his
misery. "Muthah fuckin mountains – sheeeet! Muthah fuckin rocks
– sheeeeet! Muthah fuckin snow – sheeet!"

Fear brings conflict. There are rebellions. They are organised by
the sharp black guy who I suspect is using them to cover an emotion
never felt before on the streets of his down-home ghetto, and that is
fear. He and his converts, the junkies and fundies, say I am trying to
kill them. My allies, though not by choice, are the white Southern-
ers. History, I reflect, makes fools of us all.

Early one morning we are crossing a steep mountain col, access to
which is up a steep gully. I climb up to fashion steps in hard snow
and fix some ropes to encourage the nervous. The work is tiring for I

am carrying my heavy sack. I get to the top and turn to have a rest. Below me a junkie and the sharp kid are emptying their packs of all communal gear. "No way are we going up there!" Their cries of defiance echo round the rocks. By the time I have half-run, half-glissaded down the gully they are marching off into a huge wilderness in which they will die. This time I do not reason but knock heads together while I drag my reluctant mountaineers back to their gear. It worked. We cross the col, climb down the precipice on the other side and people begin to be a bit happier. Perhaps old Kurt had something after all.

Kurt is not working for the big black lad. He continues to be miserable. I catch up with him one day while he is crossing a river called Black Creek. Up to his waist in cold snow run-off, he is muttering about being left behind and how he is going to 'sort out' the leader for the day, the boy from South Carolina. This is exactly what he does. The Southerner reacts in accordance with his beliefs – I warned you he was almost a caricature – "See," he cries, "I turn the other cheek." His transgressor is not impressed and hits it. Running out of cheeks the Southerner forgets about his beliefs and fights back. I remember I am meant to be in control of this farce and step in to bring peace. The big black lad swats me gently into the undergrowth. After repeating this tactic several times, order is restored.

My order is not restored for some time. I normally go to mountains for enjoyment. The people I normally go with feel the same way. I find it difficult to wake in beautiful places and know my companions do not share an appreciation of them. Fear and my inability to assuage it has corrupted their experience. The mountains cannot stop outside society crowding in. Then there are recriminations. The black instructor who had recruited the black lads is angry with me. He thinks I am a racist and incompetent. I think he is mad. Why did they bring tennis rackets? What did he tell them about the course and what they would be doing?

Let us leave this behind. It could get bitter. Let us talk of other things. Adventure for example. I have read that adventure in outdoor education is like painting by numbers. The essence of adventure in climbing is the uncertainty of the outcome. In outdoor education, however, the experience is so controlled by safety considerations, there can be no doubt as to the outcome and, like the numbered picture, what it will be can be seen before work commences. Outdoor adventure has to be safe. Get a reputation for killing your customers and soon you will be out of business.

I like to think that what we do is adventurous. Twenty-eight day mobile courses. Meet your group in a field. Kit them up. Give them some food and move them out. 14000 feet mountains, big wilderness terrain sometimes not even mapped properly. No base camp, no rope courses, no high wooden walls the group has to climb over to develop its solidarity, no warm baths, no served-up meals. No support, except a prearranged resupply point every eight days or so and a dime in your pocket to phone for a helicopter if things get bad. The problem is that getting out to a phone could take time. Sure, it is not the Himalayas or Alaska. It is not even the Alps. Yet it is more than enough with eight unfit tyros.

My approach is simple enough: camp as high as you can in some beautiful cirque, and select a ridge leading to an interesting peak. Even if the peak has been climbed before, the odds are against the ridge having felt the hobnail of man. Consequently there is no way of knowing what lies ahead. More often than not it turns out like a day on a bigger, more complicated and very much looser version of the Skye Ridge. So happy days are spent by students (except for the first lot) clambering up teetering towers and rappelling down on the other side, bums above great voids. I become adept at spotting ways out of trouble. Of avoiding the big afternoon lightning storms by nipping the students down gullies or discovering ramps of safe return to camp.

Then there are the rivers. These are especially dangerous early in the season, when, full of snow-melt, the terrors of their swirling depths are compounded by the presence of large tree-trunks barrelling down their courses. No painting by numbers here. If you are lucky, you find a log that has conveniently fallen over the river. If things are a bit slippy, fix a rope and the group crosses quickly. If you are unlucky, send a lookout upstream to warn of the approach of runaway logs, fix yourself on to a circle of rope and back off into the ice-cold water, hoping that if anything happens the upstream crew will remember to let go, while the downstream group pulls you in. Watching them nervously mouth your instructions to themselves as you take the plunge does not inspire confidence. "Davey, is that the downstream crew that lets go or is it...?" There is no need to worry or hope about the look-outs. If they report a log there is not much you can do except duck and that will not help a lot.

These are the landscapes of America. It is incredibly beautiful here. I am especially happy at that altitude where the forests thin out into alpine meadows full of scented wild flowers. Often we camp on some bench high in a cirque, our shelters built low and close to the scrubby pine which supports them. At night when the others finish with their talk and go to bed, I stay up to drink one more cup of tea and wonder at the sky. I have sat on many nights in many places in the mountains of the world, but this is different. The smoke from our fire drifts upwards towards a sky which is full of stars and endless space like no other night sky I have seen. In the huge silence of the void it is the perfect place to observe infinity, to conjure on its possibilities and your limitations.

Sometimes when I am on my own, after a day pulling up from some deep, forested valley in the San Juan Mountains, I am able to brush once again against the elemental forces and see a spectacular lightning storm from some position of advantage. Going off the trail and following a spur off the ridge until it seems to overhang the valley, I am able to sit like some Kerouacian Dharma Bum in a clearing and watch, on the other side, the clouds gather, dark purple and pregnant with menace over the sharp-peaked Trinity. The thunder grumbles around the peaks like some celestial choir composed of base singers only. The lightning spits at the mountain and sparks along its ridges, leaping the gaps between towers. The rain, travelling in grey vertical plates, washes down the flanks of Vestal's sculpted slabs and I am moved in a way I have never been before or since and which I cannot explain. The rain runs down my face and mixes with my tears. I taste their salt and the salt of my sweat. What will I say to the boys back home? That I saw a storm and it was so beautiful, I cried.

Today the going got bad. The mountains have been covered by a thick fog for some days now. We are at the end of this particular part of the course and we have no food left. To be resupplied we must cross the main spine of the mountains by a steep-walled col and drop down into the valley on the other side. In attempting this I am overtaken by a messenger from another group. They have a problem with a sick student.

He is lying on his side groaning. He has a pain low down on his side and he has been sick. His instructor and I think that it is appendicitis. We cannot take a risk and leave him to see if he gets better. It is a twenty mile trip down to the valley road; the first few miles desperately slow through forest deadfall before meeting the path which climbs over the ridge into the adjacent cirque. Goodness knows how much further to a telephone. If I am going to spend that dime before darkness tonight I must go now.

Down through the deadfall, quick progress frustrated by the difficult terrain. Climbing constantly up and down a jumble of fallen tree trunks, my feet and heart can find no rhythm which will reserve energy and I am worried I will not make it before nightfall. On reaching the path my spirits rise and despite the fact it climbs high over another ridge my steps quicken. Once over the ridge I, rather uncharacteristically, break into a run. Miles down the trail, just where it turns into a rough four-wheel-drive track, I have a bit of luck. Bikers out destroying the environment. As this is no occasion upon which to be sniffy, I stop one of them to explain my predicament. He takes to his white knight role with a gusto which leaves me terrified. We thunder down the trail, stones and dirt flying, my head uncomfortably close to the trees. I point out to him that while he has a helmet, I do not. Moreover, as I am the only one who knows where the sick man is, if I die so will he. He looks troubled by my cowardice but seems to slow a little.

I dismount from the bike at a small neglected-looking tavern and march boldly inside. It is packed with heavily armed men outfitted in various forms of camouflage dress. Some are wearing what to me look like Davy Crockett hats. They are hunters, massing to kill what little remains of the wildlife in the mountains. We regard each other with undisguised horror. Me, because I think I have stumbled into some kind of lynch mob determined to rid the American mountains of foreign, hippy mountaineers, and they, because I look and smell like a very disgusting foreign hippy mountaineer. Three weeks in the hills, hair matted and face black with smoke of pine fires, I realise they were more justified in their reaction than I.

No time to worry about such social niceties. I approach the bar. "Got a telephone?"

"Sure," she said, putting one up on the bar. "You got a problem?"

"Yes. I need a helicopter." Eat your heart out John Wayne!

She looks impressed and the loud talk farther up the bar quietens a little. I dial the number and give the details. They ask about a place to land and will pick me up after dropping in the doctor. I call back the bar-maid.

"Any place to land a helicopter?" The talk becomes even more muted. I put down the phone and suddenly my looks and smell do not matter so much. I am surrounded by the hunters.

"D'ya wan' a drink?"

"Holy cow!" They actually say things like this in America. "This man can call down air power!"

Thus I spend a happy hour or so drinking the hunters' beer until the sound of blades thumping through the air can be heard. They carry me to the helicopter and cheer my departure, Davy Crockett hats being thrown in the air. I look down at their up-turned faces. I am an all-American hero.

These are the days of endless summer. The time is now and I must return home. On this trip I eschew the bum-numbing Greyhound bus and travel instead to New York with an archaeologist who comes originally from dear old Glasgow – small world eh? She drives a very old black Volkswagen Karmann Ghia convertible which is not fit to cross a continent. It has bald tyres worn down to the canvas and a starter motor which does not start the engine. She also has a dog.

Our journey across America is punctuated by flat tyres, flatulance from the pooch, and embarrassing moments caused by the lack of a reliable starter motor. At one point my new-found archaeologist friend panics when she stalls the engine as we approach a tollbridge. So complete is her concentration on restarting the car, she allows it to drift by the tollbooth, from which leaps the guard, gun in hand. He is doing all this 'knees bent, both arms straight out stuff' which I thought was done only by police on the television. Is he really going to shoot us for 25 cents? I leap from the car and give him the money. He examines the coin carefully, and seemingly satisfied returns the gun to its holster.

Our peace of mind is not disturbed for long. The girl has some very nice New Mexican grass and I have bought some beer. Thus we continue on our way, driving slowly and talking of this and that. Our journey takes five days – twice as long as the bus!

On our arrival on the East Coast she takes me to a place called Peaksville, where Paul Robeson helped inaugurate the National Association for the Advancement of Coloured People. However, she has not brought me here for a lesson on American race relations. Her estranged boyfriend is out here visiting his family and she wants to make up.

My chauffeuse and her boyfriend are not to be reunited. Her hope for him slides away into the silent spaces of their halting conversation. He cannot look her in the eye. Me? I am a cynic (or perhaps a realist) and I suspect that while she has been rummaging about the dusty earth of New Mexico, rattling the bones of some ancient native, he has been rummaging about the 'co-ed dorm', rattling the bones of some contemporary native.

The trip, however, is not without some aspects of wider interest. The family of the boyfriend are a part of an interesting group of Russian Jewish socialists who had fled to America to escape the purges of Stalin, only to find themselves persecuted by McCarthy and his right-wing scoundrels. They had escaped to the hill where we find them, living first in tents before building their clapboard houses. At first the area was wilderness but after a while American-dream-suburbia grew around them – all bungalows and swimming pools. In contrast to the spruce American optimism such enclaves exude, the exiles' place had developed a certain run-down charm; the

crooked clapboard shacks mirroring the disappointment
of their owners. A people, disillusioned and displaced in
a world for which they must have had great hopes but
could not change, growing old speaking Russian and
Hebrew and going to their Sunday night dances. Is this
the reality of immigration? They remind me of my own
alien status and of journeys started in optimism,
sometimes fulfilled, sometimes not.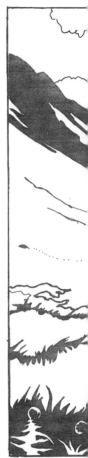

Slightly depressed, though for different reasons, we
follow the Hudson back down to New York and the
home of my chauffeuse. Compare this privilege with the
sad place we have left behind. Concrete walls and
barbed wire surround it. Inside there are marble tables,
toilets en suite, their fitments gold-encrusted. There is a
private beach and a marina. All this is guarded by a
private policeman with a large gun who comes from
Dundee. He does not like me cavorting with the
'maister's' daughter. You can see what he is thinking –
Glasgow scruff!

It is a part of that old Scottish 'Ah kent his faither'
syndrome, for he knows I am no better than he is. I do
not care. I am too busy carrying out my private fantasies,
fuelled by vicarious wealth and whiskies on the beach. I
am much more affected by another image of home. She
is an old woman who paddles in the sea, her skirts
tucked up to reveal legs lined with varicose veins. They
do not paddle in the sea on sophisticated East-coast
private beaches and when she speaks she confirms her
origins – Glasgow. This is my final reminder that I must
return home. My fantasies fade away. You are who you
are and perhaps this is what travel is all about. Not so much a
discovery of new places as it is about the discovery of yourself and
the forces that create you. The mountains of America were
wonderful but like all mountains they cannot exclude for ever the
reality of one's life and the society in which one lives that life. I
cannot stay here. My roots call me back – back to Scotland, the bogs,
the midges, the bad weather and the destructive fatalism of many of

Cir Mhor

its people. Yet, unlike the Russians, I can, and want to, return and it
is possible, even in Scotland to have days of sun and optimism. I lie
back in the warm sand and think of Arran where they paddle in
Brodick Bay and where the beautiful grey granite of Cir Mhor
beckons. The time is now. These are the days that will last for ever. I
wonder if Higgins will be free.

A Short Drive in America

Energy, they said. America has energy. It is the frontier feeling of being in command of your own fate. It is the weather that allows you to make climbing plans and does not later sabotage them. Even Scottish stoicism is replaced by that old 'get up and go'. Why then was I sitting in a wild-flower scented alpine pasture of these glorious Colorado mountains feeling awful. I had lost a serious amount of weight and my beard was becoming patchy. I had no appetite and no energy. Maybe it had something to do with the previous three months of working high in the hills providing a 'wilderness adventure experience' designed to give backbone to the traumatised young of American dream suburbia. More likely it had something to do with the freeze-dried food on which the school expected me to survive. I recall that Agnew had wrangled all summer with the articulate Outward Bound executives about it. He made no headway and we starved as the honeyed words fattened the air. With no nutrients in it known to man, this so-called food had long since stopped doing the job for which it was designed. Latterly it was coming out of my body in much the same condition as it went in. I was not happy.

But of course I was not going to lie down and die, and the next morning – a clean, sharp Colorado morning – we went down; Big Burt Redmayme, Ian 'Big Wall' Wade, Agnew (the Clydebank cowboy) and myself. We went down. Down through the meadows into the thick pine. Down to the aspens now autumnal yellow. And in them, unexpectedly, a large amount of sheep.

At the road head we waited, backs resting on packs. No one saying much. It was then he appeared. Round a curve in the trail, leading his horse by the reins; a huge ten-gallon hat and armed to the teeth; the shortest cowboy (or should it be 'sheep herd') in the world. When he drew up alongside us he stopped, swayed a little – it was six in the morning and he was drunk – and slurred "Have you seen ma sheep?" We waved our hands roughly in the direction of his sheep hoping he would go away. His guns and knives made us nervous. But he stayed, determined to make the most of the unexpected company and indulge in wee man dream games and boasts.

"Do you want to see ma pay?" He swayed again.

We said nothing.

"It's all in silver dollars. I make them give it to me in silver dollars."

And right enough, so it was. Saddle bags full of the things. He stood there swaying gently as he stretched himself to his limit in order to raise flaps of the bags. There was a look of determined satisfaction on his face. There, that will show these strangers that he is someone to be reckoned with. Why does he do it? There does not seem to be an answer. Some sad variation on his dream-world, wild-west fantasy perhaps. We tried to show just the right amount of interest in case he shoots us for being too interested, or for not being interested enough. We said very little.

Perhaps for this reason he appeared to tire of us, for he gathered the reins of his horse and shuffled away round the corner of the trail and out of sight, all the time muttering to himself about 'godarn' men without horses. In the silence he left behind, I laid back on my pack trying to put my heart back into normal order. Perhaps it was my lethargy but it all seemed surreal; almost an 'Alice through the looking glass' world. I was too tired to think much sense into it. In retrospect it seems clear. The 'sheep herd', some remnant of the older, more traditional ways of using the mountains confronted by the new. He probably thought of us as representatives of those critics who argued that sheep grazing did horrendous ecological damage to the delicate Colorado mountains. At the time I was too weak to bother and only one weary thought trundled through my head. Why does he not ride his horse? Is he too wee to mount it unaided?

Energy slowly returned. First in the long breakfasts taken outdoors to enjoy those clear, keen Colorado mornings, the very sharpness of them sensed in your nostrils. The oblique light shining through forest mists. A deep silence broken only by the flicking magpies in the meadows. Later, there is another energy-giving period up in the hills as we sit under our sodden tarps waiting for the return of our students, delayed by a nasty Rocky Mountain-wide snow storm.

It was during that time that Wade began to construct roads of possibilities in my mind. What was I going to do now? Going home, but I have nine days before I must catch my plane in New York. Yosemite? ("It'sa long way tago for a few days' climbing"). Wade has some business in Jackson Hole (big plans involving setting up a climbing school in the Wind Rivers) before we can go. But why not, and why not, when we are up in Wyoming, swing into the Winds and do something there. Big Burt and Wade had their eye on something on Haystack, and the last time we had been in the Cirque of Towers doing the big steep route on Pingora, I had taken a fancy to the North Face of Mount Mitchell. Yes, we can take Chuck. He was looking for a lift to Sacramento. Yes, the energy had returned.

Chuck was interesting. A hippy with long hair, beads and studied Californian coolness. It was 1970 after all. He had little climbing experience, but a lot of good balance and was used to going carefully in high places. He was a high-wire walker looking to break into the circus. He was never without the tackle that stretched his wire rope between two trees. At breakfast on the back porch of the lodge, or in the early evening, he could be seen practising by walking up the wire of the ski-tow behind the lodge, long balance pole in hand. Every now and again he would purposefully fall off so that he could practise catching the wire and pulling himself up again. More 'Alice through the looking glass'. Chuck would climb alright. I would just have to check his belays.

And so we set off. Ian, Chuck and I, and Chuck's little dog, in Ian's big old Falcon van. We will meet Burt up there. This time no 'Alice through the looking glass', just wild 'Kerouac on the road' fantasies:

> We sat tight and bent our minds to the goal. We went over Berthoud Pass, down to the great plateau, Tabernash, Trouble-some, Kremmling; down Rabbit Ears Pass to Steamboat Springs,

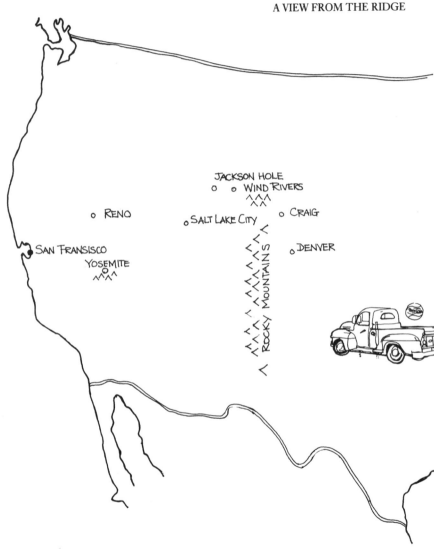

JACKSON HOLE
o   o WIND RIVERS

o RENO

o SALT LAKE CITY

o CRAIG

SAN FRANSISCO

o DENVER

YOSEMITE

ROCKY MOUNTAINS

Short Drive in America

and out; fifty miles of dusty detour; then Craig and the Great American Desert.

Movement charged us with energy but at Craig we stopped. There is a restaurant called 'Brown's Working Man's Café' in which we ate cheap meats and beers served by a grey lined-faced waitress. She drawled a tired parody of the Western waitress welcome, "What are ya havin' today boys?" Outside like some eternal American cliche the neon sign flashed, illuminating in the dusk the dusty Craig streets, decaying clapboard houses and some large trees, brown leaves scattered around their roots. The streets were empty. The town seemed tired, lost and sad, yet, with my mind smoothed by alcohol, I was happy. I was living my American Dream. With the ghost of Kerouac I was on the road, searching for the source of Neal Cassady's (his hero, both in real life and many of his books, including *On The Road*) energy behind the drab homogenising strips of gas stations and hamburger franchises. I was younger then and thus did not realise that it eluded me, as it had Kerouac. There was so much energy going through me in huge courses of adrenalin that I was ready to accept my idealisation as reality. With wild whooping cries we slipped into the gloaming.

It was dark when we crossed the high Wyoming desert plateau. We grew quieter. It was that vast, empty and mysterious place which reduces the chatter of men to silence. The harvest moon, so large and so close you could have reached out and grabbed it to give to a loved one. It was low down in a sky which was so big and clear that it did not seem to be the same sky which covers old Europe. And as with Kerouac a litany of small towns; Rock Springs, Reliance, Eden, Farson and Boulder. As we passed through each one I looked at the clusters of buildings, darkened save for the odd light and felt a strange disorientation – a shiver of confused culture-shock. What real American lives were lived here? It was difficult to avoid the cliches of film and book as I peered, polar minded, into the darkness, trying to discern reality in the outlines of the low buildings and the dust of the streets. Was it Harper Lee's small town America of *To Kill a Mocking Bird*, where the wise lawyer and the fearless editor defend the rights of all men? Or did the darkness conceal a harsher truth of slow-witted and obese hicks whose narrow lives spawn narrow minds, suspicious of all outsiders? I was to get some kind of answer to my questions a few days later.

At Boulder we turned off the road and drove for forty miles of dusty dirt track, past silent ranches, silver-roofed in the moonlight and I remembered our last time there. Lost in the tumbleweed desert, we had dossed down under that huge clear sky and watched the shooting-stars overtake the satellites. In the morning we were awakened by a bright red sky which would have made the wee 'sheep herd' back in Colorado pause for thought.

This time there were no false turns. We went swiftly and confidently over the drumming trail to reach, at last, Big Sandy. There to ease stiff bodies out of the van to sleep under the pines among squirrels and chipmunks; and no bears, we hoped.

After a day's walk and another night in the open, this time in the last of the trees just under the summit of Jackass Pass, we left for the North Face of Mount Mitchell to the sound of Chuck's dog barking at the unfairness of being tied to a tree to await our return. We had other things on our mind. It was cold and there were some dark clouds about. We were rather too lightly clad for a storm like the one which had held up our students a few days earlier. I was not too bad in light sweater and anorak, but Chuck looked like he was going for a stroll down Main Street Sacramento in jeans and a tee shirt.

Such anxiety always seems to give the adrenalin surge an extra injection for soon I was motoring my way up the initial grooves. They were not too hard, yet someone had had a problem for at the top of each of the first four pitches was a nice new Lost Arrow piton and abseil sling. In true Scots fashion I removed them and put them in my pack so as to have no argument as to their ownership.

After these initial steep pitches, the way was up a series of the finest granite corners I have ever had the pleasure to climb. Absolutely clean dihedrals of lovely rough, grey stuff complete with holds. For the first time on granite, it seemed that I did not have to thrutch up cracks or heave myself up holds spaced for an eight-foot being. It was a sheer delight to soar up this face. Pitch after pitch of trouble-free climbing. Chuck, with all his high-wire experience took to the climbing, as I had anticipated, with great ease. He even led through and, with the exception of one or two belays where the nuts swivelled a little in their cracks, was technically very safe.

It was so relaxing I had time to recall what had been said to me about Chouinard on the first ascent. Seemingly he and his party, anticipating a great struggle, had set off with all the accoutrements for a multi-day ascent. Despite being thus encumbered they still reached the summit that day.

Of course, as any climber will tell you, when everything is going so well there is bound to be a problem. Ours came on reaching the bowl that dominates the last quarter of the face. We had seen no evidence of the big storm which had delayed our students a few days earlier. The cracks and walls had been free of ice and snow, and although it had been cold the dark clouds of the morning had come to nothing. The bowl, however, was filled with steep soft snow, pitched at an angle which hinted at the possibility of downward movement. Consequently, with great care I waded diagonally leftwards and upwards to the bottom of the chimney/crack which provided access to the top part of the face. To my horror, it was filled with ice and I was wearing PA's – a smooth-soled, lightweight summer boot.

There was little else to do but cut some steps with my peg hammer to allow access to a dark, cold recess where a belay was found. Chuck followed quickly, and blue with cold, hurried to tackle the next pitch. The ice slowed us down but we managed to cope, sometimes cutting steps, sometimes bridging, until we reached a wall capped by a large overhang. The way lay to the right by a steep wall, adorned only with a few large hollow-sounding flakes. They were the kind of things you look at from the bottom of a pitch thinking to yourself – they don't look so good, no way am I going to use them – only to find yourself, five minutes later, swinging from them, thinking – well they are all you've got, so maybe they are alright after all. The wall turned out to be the final pitch. With one last heave on one such dubious flake, we were able to warm ourselves in the late afternoon sunshine on the summit. Chuck's first major climb as an independent mountaineer had been absolutely superb; he had enjoyed himself but not enough to distract him from his high-wire walking. Conscious of the long walk out and the many miles to Yosemite, we did not linger long on the top. Time only for a quick appreciation of the peaks of the Cirque – the serrated tops of War Bonnet, the elegant sweep of the flank of Wolf's Head and the steep-walled Pingora – before swooping down to Jackass Pass and a wild barking welcome.

The next day we stopped at Pinedale, a cow town on the road to Jackson Hole, where some of the questions I had been asking myself a few nights earlier were answered. In a country where waitresses meet you with a warmth designed to make you feel that you have made their day by sitting at their table, the one in the diner we chose for lunch was strangely hostile. As she had greeted our request for beer with a surly jerk of the head towards the adjacent bar, I went through to get some. There my longish hair, sandals and shorts drew unfavourable comments from the two sole customers. Did they not tar and feather strangers who came to their town in shorts and sandals and looked like foreign hippies, they drawled to one another. They could talk, for they looked like a couple of desperadoes from a cowboy film, all ten-gallon hats and winkle-picker, high-heeled boots. I summoned up my best John Wayne look and without waiting to argue, collected the beer and hurried back to the restaurant. That was Pinedale, Wyo., a town where they liked to beat up climbers. Not unlike Lochranza, Arran, really.

After hurried, big climbing business in Jackson Hole, we left at night taking turns to sleep in the back of the van. It was into Idaho then out across the last western fragments of the Rockies, down the canyons to Salt Lake City. Then by white Bonneville flats across the

Mid-America

great desert into Nevada, cowboy music on every radio station, to sleep, stationary this time, in a super toiletted lay-by outside Reno. In the morning 'Alice' came back. We had breakfast in some big casino served by women whose breasts were barely restrained by tiny dresses and whose legs were encased in fish net stockings. Along with our bacon and eggs they tried to sell us bingo cards. Downstairs, people, their eyes on stalks, played rows of fruit machines. They looked as if they had been there all night fretting with a fortune which was in their minds only.

Reno was no place for us innocents. We slipped away quietly on the huge freeways, past the little chapels by the desert, where the quickly divorced can just as quickly put themselves back into another decaying relationship, into the desert, the dust and the heat.

Sacramento came quickly. There Chuck disappeared out of our lives. Through the harsh smog-encrusted early afternoon light he dodged expertly through eight lanes of freeway madness. On his back an old battered and holey Millet sack which I had given him. He was delighted with it – "It don't make me look like no greenhorn." His little dog led the way, straining at the rope leash. He had had enough of mountains and snow. He could smell home and comfort. He hopped over the last barrier followed by Chuck. A final wave, a shout we did not hear over the noise of the traffic, and he was gone for ever.

It was still light, just when we arrived at Yosemite. Passing through the gates of El Capitan and the Cathedrals it was all very familiar – I recalled the hours staring at the Ansel Adams' photographs – yet it was completely new. We camped at Camp Four, big macho climbers' camp, and the next day we were off to Glacier Apron to do some Harding route. It went like 'Hammer' on the Etive Slabs; long lay-backs with delicate little slabby moves for variety.

Back at Camp Four some Yosemite realities began to impose themselves. A girl undermined any lingering sense of achievement when she enquired as to what we had done that day. The grade did not impress her and she responded with disgust. "Jeee-sus I can do that!" So it did not look like we were going to 'get laid'.

Then there was the gentle noise of tinkling chrome molly. Like mobiles made out of climbing iron, this soporific sound lulled you to sleep at night, and was there when you rose in the morning. It was the sound of big-wall men packing their haul bags. Completion of the packing did not necessitate a move to climb. There would then follow a period of what was called 'getting your head together'. This seemed to consist of sitting in yoga positions in front of the haul bags as if they were altars, muttering wee prayers called mantras. Sometimes the waiting climbers consulted the *I Ching* as to their approaching destiny. Was it an auspicious time to go? Would there be a storm? Would the enterprise be successful? The answers to these questions would be sought in the interpretation of the often ambiguous explanations of hexagrams chosen fortuitously by the toss of coins. Thus hours were spent trying to wrest meaning from the wise writings. "The fifth six, divided, shows its subject shooting a pheasant. He will lose his arrow, but in the end he will obtain praise and obtain a (high) charge." The climbers would incantate, solemnly reading from the book. A pause for thought, followed by this. "Gee, hey, outasight, right-on man. We're goin ta make it man, but we're goin to lose our peeetons. Shit! We can't lose our peetons man! Try it again man!"

There was a strange contradiction among some of these American climbers. On the one hand was their energy and rational know-how. These things manifested themselves in the development of magnificent equipment and programmes of training and planning. However, alongside this sense of practicality was their indulgence in the mysticism of Transcendental Meditation and the fatalism of *I Ching*. While it is true that the claims of TM to improve one's physical and mental performance, sit easily with American individualism, it seemed that it was not just enough to go and climb. One must have some deeper pseudo-religious purpose, or pseudo-psychological self-actualisation in the experience to justify the activity; a manifestation of some deep American presbyterian guilt, suffered when you might be doing something useless yet enjoyable? Something we Scots can recognise without difficulty. Whatever the causes 'getting your head together' took a long time, for men thus engaged when we arrived, were still at it when we left four days later.

The next day was a bit of a waste. We tried a climb but whether it was a reaction to the travelling or the heat, I did not feel good enough. So we came down and wandered around looking at all the big climbs Wade had done. The 'Nose', North America Wall, and the second ascent of the South-east Face of Half Dome are among the most notable. The latter was done with Scots climber 'Bugsy' McKeith. A teeter on 'Bat Hooks' and a big storm that enforced a prolonged bivouac is Wade's story to tell.

He probably will not tell it for he is the quietest of Englishmen. Not given to rushing into print at the drop of a piton, Ian had done the first British ascents of these big climbs, unknown to the contemporary glitterati of **Mountain Magazine**.

Ian's big strength was his aid climbing. Ignorant of such things. I had, in my prejudiced ways, always thought aid climbing was a bit of a grunt. In Ian's case it was an elegant activity, parsimonious of energy. Seldom was there a wasted movement. He would assess the placement, select without failure the correct piece of gear, have it in and stand on it in much the same time it took me to describe it.

I have not much memory of the last climb we did in Yosemite. It was on Middle Cathedral and it took two days. It was steep and strenuous, thrutching around in deep chimneys with a lot of aid. It was the kind of climbing that does not require much thought, for there is not much in the way of alternatives; no searching for the subtle hold that suddenly brings you into balance and makes the upward move inevitable. There you are presented with a problem to which there is but one solution, usually strenuous, and often, jamming.

Two things, however, stand out undimmed by the passing of all these years. The first was the incident of the two bolts – or more accurately, the incident of the one bolt where two should have been. Wade was some way above me doing his speedy stuff on a particularly blank-looking bit of granite when he groaned, "Someone has smashed the top bolt. I can't reach the next placement." There was, of course, only one solution. I would have to climb up, clip into the bottom and remaining bolt while Ian climbed up onto my shoulders to execute the next move.

I was not acquainted with bolts, and aware of the 1000 feet void at my heels. I eyed this one with something less than enthusiasm. Both our weights were on it, and it was the handiwork of some American craftsman unknown to me. "Are these things alright?" I asked, trying not to sound like an absolute poltroon. Wade with one foot in the small of my back was making the difficult high mantleshelf with the other on to my shoulder. He had the fingers of one hand in my mouth and those of the other, in my eyes. I was not comfortable. "Sure," he replied, confident though breathing heavily. "But sometimes they get loose through weathering." A weak "Oh," was all I could manage in reply.

'Alice' again. This is crazy I thought. Look at all the modern gear we have and yet here we were reduced to the earliest of all techniques – combined tactics. We could be any one of a number of doughty pioneers who had used it on the Mantrap of the North-east Buttress of Ben Nevis. No matter. Wade was now skipping off my unhelmeted head onto the lower rung of his etrier. Well at least he was not wearing tricounis.

The second and most compelling memory was of a terrible thirst occasioned by strenuous climbing in what to me was unbearable heat. (And this was on the north side of the valley.) At the bivouac, along with the paranoia of dropping my boots into the void, I spent a restless night with my tongue sticking to my palate, my dreams interrupted by overflowing pints of McEwan's Export. At the top it was worse. Now exposed to the full force of the sun, we had to make our way through an almost impenetrable gorse-like plant, over the summit of Upper Cathedral, before being able to descend a gully to the valley floor. Weak from the effects of dehydration it seemed to take me for ever. But at the bottom there was Ian with a gallon jar of 'Wylers'. I disposed of the lot; some even got in my mouth.

It was beginning to come to an end. I sat with another gallon jar as we dropped down out of the valley to Merced on our way to San Francisco. Here is some others' reality. An evil 'Alice', an uncomfortable counterpoint to the beautiful valley we had just left. The skies around this town were black with the exhausts of the B52 bombers which seem to be landing and taking off continuously. The last pieces to be played in the mad end-game which will destroy us in order to save us, they seem to hover over the town like hunchbacked vultures. The paranoia of small-town America transferred to the world stage.

In cosmopolitan San Francisco they were quickly forgotten. There we rode the trams, had a big lobster dinner on Fisherman's Wharf and got drunk in the airport before I caught the 'red eye' for New York. I drank water through the night and all the next day across the Atlantic, but the thirst was still on me. The last act of the stewardess before she hurried to her seat for the descent into Glasgow was to get me a drink of water.

I do not know how many miles it is from San Francisco to Glasgow, but I had plenty of time to think about the previous nine days. I thought about the 'sheep herd', the small towns, the gamblers, the desert, the mountains and most of all, the energy. I had returned from the land of the dreamers, and it was often difficult to separate reality from myth, truth from idealisation. However to dream there meant optimism, energy and action; action limited only by one's own resources, be they material, physical or psychological. I was coming home to hope that such dreams could be sustained in the face of energy dissipated in the search for a living, love and climbs in fickle Scottish weather. But I realised that these Scottish barriers did not matter, for as long as one goes to the hills, one is always coming home. It is unimportant if the hills are old friends or newly-awaited delights hidden by the dark of a night march. It is that familiar feeling of anticipation experienced regardless of whether one is walking into the twilight of a Scottish evening in Glen Affric under copper-bottomed clouds, or of whether one is crossing the high Wyoming plateau. It sometimes seems they are the only real and true things beyond which all else is nothing. Even twenty years on the expectations thus raised bring forth their own optimism and hence, energy.

Shenavall

Big, Black-Hairtet River

I kent fine that auld memories wid be steered, auld broken links jined up, auld freendships and hostilities bleeze intae life. Even afore the buik appeared spierin for foties and information awoke curiosity, led tae promises tae meet again. Tae a shot at the darnin o' worn claith.

I picked up Mealy Puddin fae his hoose in a douce Auld Reekie street, spikkin tae his bonnie loons fan I waited. They've nae interest in the hill, he telt me, and neither hae the rest o' yon crowd's progeny. Like Mealie's, Stumpy's and Desperate Dan's bairns think they're daft sleepin under steens. He disnae hae muckle contact wi them noo; they seldom leave Aiberdeen nooadays. But this time we were pickin up Stumpy at Inverness station and headin for Shenevall and, hopefully, An Teallach.

It was Mey and braw weather, so we wis dumfounnert by the blizzard at Braemore. And we'd the bendy beets and nae axes or crampons. We waitet in the pub for it tae get better; it didnae. They buy their ain drink; I'd forgotten that.

"Is't far tae this bothy?" Stumpy askit fan we startit. Ye mind tell o' him, the engineer? Fit's he daein noo? Weel, he wis aye collectin junk an takkint hame. I mind he took a piece o' airoplane hame fae Beinn Eighe for his muntelpiece, till somebiddy pyntet oot that was a bane in it! Throw it awa? Nivver, he wis ower ticht fistit; he probably made soup oot o't. So he's a museum curator noo. Suits him, gets pyed for collectin junk. I telt him it would tak aboot an oor.

It wisnae ower bad at first and we blethered, as the snaw fell, aboot the buik; they spiered, made suggestions. I askit aboot Dan, and Stumpy says, "He's in America. Naw, he's still nae workin, he'll nivver work noo. Still lives aff the wife. Na, he's nae climbin ony mair except ontae the bar stool. He's aboot fifteen steens! Mind the time he was oot wi Strange, askin fit a' his gear wis for. Pickin up nuts, crabs and the like? And then he picket up the haunle o' his dixie and askit, 'Fit's this for', 'For the wee cracks' came back the answer. He wis richt mad fan abody laughed their heids aff! Pit that in yer buik."

Aifter an oor we came tae the fork in the path far the track tae Shenavall gings aff tae the richt, snakein roon the base o' An Teallach afore fa'in tae Strath na Sealga. Torches cam oot as the blizzard got waur and the pucklie stars disappeared.

"It's a bit further than I thocht," I said.

There wisnae muckle said as we stummelt on in the blizzard alang a path that was mair glaur nor dry grund. Aifter a while we couldnae follae the path amang the heather and boulders. It was mirk dark and I took oot the compass tae get a bearing tae Strath na Sealga. It wis a' a bit like yon poem, the three o' us,

> A cold coming we had of it,
> Just the worst time of the year
> For a journey, and such a long journey:
> . . . . . .
> With the voices singing in our ears, saying
> That this was all folly.
> (Eliot *Journey of the Magi*).

"Foo will we find the bothy in this licht?" said Stumpy. That was the least o' my worries; gettin aff the hill wis the priority. The snaw was driftin noo and we crawled roon boulders by torch-licht. Tae the desperate e'e darkness is nae a unform state; ye ken yersel hoo on the hill there are shades o' black that ye strain for? The black curtain hingin fae the sky was searched for the tiniest rent and then I saw a slate-grey blackness tae the richt. Loch na Sealga. The grund began tae fa awa.

"The bothy's doon there; aboot twenty minutes," I said, trying tae sound as if I was nivver worriet. I kent, by the trees in the torchlicht, that we were near and by the less rocky grund. But till we touched the wa's wi wir fingers we couldnae see it.

Inside, knackered, Stumpy comments, "I mind noo, hoo I stopped daein this!"

He wis aye a cheery loon. At least till he got belted by yon bobby

o'er the heids o the Queen. I hiv telt ye the story, the ane at Crathie
Kirk! Weel, listen, and ye'll hear noo. We'd been in mony a stramash
thegither, dangled aff mony a rope and focht in mony airts wi the
maisters o' war but this maun hae been the tichtest neuk.

Gettin the poles in the bus wis the hardest thing; we near pyked
oot the driver's e'en. But are ye sure I've nae telt ye this story? No,
it's nae the same ane as the set-tae at Gelder Shiel but anither ane
aboot the Queen. Ye're sure, richt ye are then!

This wis in the dark ages fan there wis still coal fires and fires o'
idealism in the youth. We were a' that delighted in '64 fan Harald
fae Huddersfield defeated the class enemy that had ruled a' wir lives
but that seen faded. Wage freezes, keeping the bomb, and abune a',
support for the Yankees in Vietnam, seen made HIM the enemy. So
we focht tae arouse the fires o' revolutionary fervour in the local
proletariat; leaflets, torchlicht marches, bomb hoaxes on Yankee
ships in the harbour, that kind o' thing. Burned a Yank flag on the
Edzell air base and near got thrawn for it.

Weel, a' this took time and the hills took a back place for a while.
Then Stumpy I think it wis, hid the idea o' mixin duty wi pleesure.
He, Harald, wid be at Balmoral tae see the Queen; we'd plot his
Hastings for him and combine a day on the hill wi agitprop. The
banner wis nae problem; it said something like **STOP SUPPORT-
ING US AGGRESSION IN VIETNAM.** But the poles, that wis
the problem, baith on and aff the bus and then up tae the doss. We
decidet Gelder wis o'er obvious; there'd probably be bodyguards
aboot and how wid we explain the poles?

So we sleekit past Invercauld and made for the Secret Howff on
Beinn a' Bhuird; naebody wid come across us there. We trudged up
the glen wi the poles slung o'er oor shulders, like African bearers
wantin their leopard. And for a wee whylie the next day, fan the
napalm and agent orange aye rained doon, wir banner fluttered its
message across the hills ootside the howff. Then we stashed it awa
and went up the hill, tae dae some desperate diff. That wis aboot wir
standard fan Dan wisnae there.

I canna mind fit we did. It wis something up in Coire na Ciche but
oor minds were on the morn and we were seen doon again tae the

doss. We realised we'd nae watch atween us and feared sleepin in on Sunday morning, so we decidet tae ging doon and doss ootside the Kirk that nicht. We packet up and went back doon tae the road, startet wakkin alang tae Crathie, a guid few mile. A larry-driver stopped and gied us a lift. Fan we telt the him we were for Crathie, he startet tellin's that they had transvestite orgies in Balmoral. We tried tae broaden his critique o' monarchy ontae mair o' a revolutionary position but he wis only interestet in the orgies.

We kipped doon at the bus shelter jist ablow the Kirk and got the stoves oot for wir tea. I wis jist steering the beans fan Stumpy said, "Dinna look up but there's a Bobby comin taewards us." And alang he came. I tried tae look unconcerned as he spake.

"Hello, lads, and fit'll ye be daeing here?"

I stirred a little, then ansert. "We've missed the bus, got doon o'er late fae the hill. We'll get the first ane the morn."

He lookit at us, seeing the combat jackets, sandals, Stumpy's Fidel Castro beard. Hippies, beatniks, you could bynear hear him thinking. Hitchin aboot the countra we'd been run in afore for oor looks and spent a nicht in the jyle. But he'd ither things on his mind.

"Weel, mind and be gone early. The Queen is coming tae Kirk at 11 o'clock and ye'd better nae still be here then!"

We assured him that we'd remove wir offendin carcases lang afore that and he left.

Of course we slept in, were still sleeping fan the same bobby appeart again, angry this time, in the shelter.

"Get up the pair o' ye and get oot o' my sicht! Get yer gear thegither or I'll run ye in!"

We lookit oot o' wir sleeping bags; the road was jammed wi people. Loyal, patriotic citizens oot for a Sunday picnic and tae see the Queen. We'd missed Harald, he wis inside the Kirk.

Muttering apologies under his glower we obeyed the bobby and packet, athoot breakfast. He watched us as we moved awa doon the road till, satisfied, he returned tae his duty o' keepin patriotic fervour athin reasonable bounds. We walkit in silence for a while then, "Fit noo?" fae Stumpy.

"Foo lang dae these services last?"

"Aboot an oor; they finish in time for denner."

"Richt, we'll hide oor packs, get the banner ready, and rush up fan we see them comin oot."

Wi' heavy hairts the packs were deposited ahind a tree, the banner attached tae the poles.

"Funny the bobby didnae notice the poles," mused Stumpy, as he slippit the banner on. We rolled it up sae as tae rush through the crowd. But as time went by wir courage ebbed. We were baith silently hopin we'd missed them fan a cheer rose fae the crowd. I wis still hesitatin fan Stumpy surged forret on his lane, so I tried tae catch him up afore the first cars went past. But as I reached him on the kerbstane I saw King Harald and Lizzie gae by, gieing wee daft waves at Stumpy. And I noticed as weel the bobby, across the road, comin taewards us. Then anither car cam slowly doon the brae.

"Quick Stumpy, there's anither ane," I cried and unfurled the end o' the banner and we baith moved ontae the road and stood in front o' it. It wis the Queen mither that we'd stopped.

Pandaemonium! That wis the only word tae describe it. Dizzens o' sleepy photographers wakkint up and we were dazzled wi the flashes o' cameras. Wee wifies rushed at Stumpy an cloured him wi their handbags. Some folk threw steens at him! And then the big bobby appeared, flung Stumpy agin a tree and started layin aboot him. Wallop, wallop! And that wis the funny thing, naebody pyed ony attention tae me. I suppose I should hae rushed tae his rescue bit I jist stood there, stunned like.

Then it stopped. The bobby stopped beltin him and held the wee wifies back. He hissed, "Get the hell oot o' here. If ye're here in twa minutes, ye're nicked!"

Weel, we didnae need telt twice. So we rolled up the banner and sleekit awa.

The next day we were on the front page o' ilka newspaper in the land and in the Yankee anes forbye. Or rather Stumpy wis, wi the banner and an airm o' me. He definitely stole the show. And the funny thing wis, shortly aifter, fan the Yankees bombed Hanoi,

Harald said he couldnae support it. Noo I'm nae claimin a' the credit for that but surely it's o'er muckle o' a coincidence tae be jist that?

But tae get back tae Shenavall, we'd gotten there, onywyes. Fit did we dae? Weel, that was a bit o' a disaster. We wakkint tae fool weather the next day; cloud, rain, a smirr o' sleet. We decidet against An Teallach, leavin't for the morn, and tae dae the Fisherfield Munros at t'ither side o' the river.

We couldnae cross the river.

It flowed huge and savage tae the loch. Deep, its banks o'erflowed at mony points. It wis an invitation tae a wattery grave. We wakkit upstream seekin a ford. Fower miles we wakkit, tae Loch an Nid, and still we couldnae cross yon river.

Weet? We were sypit, drookit; miserable. We trailed back doon tae the bothy and half wye fun an abandont cottage. Ye ken it? Achneigie? Murray wis there aifter the war and there was still a faimily intilt, wi' a teacher, if I mind richt. Onywye, it wis open and in we went. There wis timmer a-plenty ootside and auld papers inside. We seen had a bleeze goin and Mealy fund a kettle, dried milk and tea bags, and got a brew on. Then he pullt an auld transistor fae his pooch and we were seen listenin tae the Dons against the Gers. Fa won? I canna mind. A draw, I think.

We bade there a while, Mealy wi his fitba, Stumpy readin a pile o' auld car magazines, drying oorsels oot by the fire. Stumpy wintet tae bide there – ye ken foo they like best tae be on their lane up there? It's nae exactly that they are nae freendly; it's jist that an Aiberdonian's nivver fun onybody worthy of his company, yet.

But we went back tae Shenavall. Tae anither fire far mony hid gaithered aifter a disappintin day. There was a big crood roon the fire and we had the drams and chat.

"Far's the young folk," I cried, "Look around ye, it's a' folk like us, wi wrinkles and bags under the e'en. They're aff skiin and snorkelling and fit like. Thatcher's bairns, nae depth, weel-adjusted and tae a philistine society. Nae passion, nae ideas."

That got them startet aff but Stumpy jist sat there quaet-like, said nivver a word. And Mealy Puddin wis snorin!

The next day we tried An Teallach, got up tae the ridge. But the wind blew o'er the verglas and cracked cornices. And we'd nae ice axes, forbye my wakkin-stick that we passed up and doon on the snaw slope tae the ridge, like yon Gorgons at the back o' the north wind, passin the yin e'e atween them. So we descended tae the bothy.

Afore leavin, we took foties.

"Let's immortalise the designer babygro on ye Stumpy. Nivver thocht we'd see ye in the salopants."

And in the foties we're a' smilin.

Hiv I been oot wi' them again? Nae wi Stumpy. But I got a letter fae Mealie sayin the book minded him of 'those happy days' fan we were loons. And that's queer since he wis aye soor-faced fan I kent him. But then we were sellin nostalgia and he maun hae a great need o' nostalgia wi his mid-life crisis and designer diseases. He aye catches fit's fashionable; it's Coxackie B the noo.

So we went tae Gortan, he'd nae been there. That wis anither disaster. He took some fushionless lad wi him, picked up God kens whaur and we wakked in on a bonny starry nicht, snaw doon on the path. We could see the ridge o' hills intended for the morn. But in the morning the mist was doon and by 10.00 it was blawing a blizzard. The spindrift wis blawing stoor on the taps so we traipsed back tae the car. We near went intae the ditch a puckle times afore Tyndrum and then the windscreen wipers broke. Mealy had tae louse his lacers and tie them tae the blades, pullin like a wabster so we could see oot.

Ony ithers? Jist Fishgut Mac the twa times. He still sings, in a pub in Inverness. Went there tae see him. Apart fae the plug in his guitar it could hae been 20 year ago. Ye ken fit I mean? Up the merry plooboys and doon wi' the maisters o' war. Great. Disnae get on the hill much, femily and that.

We went up Sgurr nan Clach Geala. Mind, ye ging past Braemore and then up a widded glen, wi waterfalls and a big cliff leadin up tae Beinn Dearg on the richt-han side? Fae the tap we could see a' the peaks o' Sutherland. Mac wis pechan on the wye up but he fairly beat me doon; I think he fair enjoyed the day.

We steered o'er auld times and freens. Maist are either intae middle-aged cauldrife lives, or lumpenised. Some are deid. We despaired o' the youth o' the day. Fit we thocht were permanent changes wernae; The Times Didnae Change. The tae lot hae kirk waddins, the tither look for oblivion. Maks ye feart.

> O wae's me on the weary days
> When it is scarce grey licht at noon;
> It maun be a' the stupid folk
> Diffusin' their dullness roon and roon
> (MacDiarmid *To Circumjack Cencrastus*)

Aboot a year later we went up Strathconon; a bonny glen, but naething but geriatrics and white settlers there noo. We were headed for Maoile Lunndaidh.

A big river ran atween us an wir mountain but the path was on this side o' the river. So we crossed wi the brig and did athoot the path. Fower oors oot, fower oors back. Deep heather, saft snaw, dubs; it wis murder. Mac tried tae droon himsel a couple o' times on the wye oot, in the side burns but didnae manage. On the wye back somebody had deepened the burns, dug up the grun and streetched the path oot. Mac accused me o' tryin tae kill him. But aifter a couple o' pints he forgave me. I took him haim. He tried tae donate me his anarchist library; I suggestit he gie it tae a University and listent tae a few o' the auld sangs and went haim.

Baith Mealy and Mac sent tapes for the loon, ye ken, kiddie's sangs; them baith bein faithers themsels. And I did get across the river wi' Mealy, fan we did Beinn Mhanach ae winter's day, him bewailing the balance o' class forces, and recedin prospects for civil war. So mebbe ye can get across yon river, if ye want till hard eneuch. It minds me o' fit yon aul mannie said tae me in Harris, aboot guid men comin fae Aiberdeen and the better men comin oot o' it. Ye get my meaning? Na, weel, nivver mind.

My pairtner in crime's pals? Weel, I dinna richt ken bit for the anes I met mysel. There wis Al. The Stobcross Gentlemen's

Climbing Club had booked the C.I.C. Hut and invited Al, fa hidnae been there for twenty year, and had never pyed for it fan he wis. He and Davie are mentioned in yon Crocket buik on Nevis, as the anes fa's contribution wis tae develop new wyes o' gettin intae the hut athoot pying. They pit the bars on tae keep them oot. Bides up on Donside noo, unsuperannuated, switchin on the car lichts and runnin doun mountain hares fan he needs a few bob. But haein a revival, gettin tae the Alps and America, daein hard things.

He hauled me up a couple of V.Diffs, or rather sax bits o' sax different anes since he disnae haud wi guide books, afore daeing Raeburn's Arête wi' Davy. Fan they come back a couple o' youngsters, loon and quine, super-fit and stripey panted cam doon fae Bullroar on Carn Dearg, full o' themsels and a wee bit deprecatin o' the auld men daeing auld routes.

"I did thae routes on Carn Dearg when they were hard," came back Al, and the youngsters e'en widened as they chatted o' Higgins and Cunningham and ithers fae the past. Aye, he showed them tae respect their elders.

But he didnae like the idea o' the buik. These things shouldnae be written doon. You did them for intrinsic worth, nae fame or lucre. Even if anonymity meant loss of record and memory. Tae him it wis an extension o' the regular jobs, mortgages and pensions o' the Stobcross Gentleman's Club members. Like Hogg's mither tae Walter Scott fan he prentet her sangs, Al felt 'Ye've spyled it a!'

There wis an official reunion, a party tae celebrate. Aboot a dizzen o' us went tae A'Chuil bothy, cartin in coal by the hunnerweicht and drink by the gallon. We had a fine day up Sgurr na Ciche, follyin the dyke back in the spindrift tae Garbh Chioch Mhor and back tae the doss tae roast and toast in the glow o' polite praise. Maist were recent freens but ane wis an auld-timer cried Erchie Boomer, a kenspeckle figure fae Luss tae the Fort and ayont. He wis wild, a bit like the Wild Man o' Borneo. Wearin tattered clais, breeks at half mast, wild tufts o' hair stickin oot fae his bauldy heid, his poppy eyes glowin as he telt and re-telt tales that split yer sides. He seemed tae hae naething in his rucksack but drink; a dizzen cans o' beer, and then somebody took oot a tin, "I've got a pheasant – tae celebrate, like."

Back comes Erchie quick as a flash, "I've got a brace o' grouse!" – and oot o' his sack comes twa bottles o' the amber nectar o' the same name. Somebiddy took oot the posh cheese, the Swiss stuff wi the holes intilt.

"The man wi the lightweight cheese, wi the holes drilled in!" cries the Boomer, and so forth. Ye'll hae tae get Erchie tae tell ye his ain tales o' the Purvis brothers and ithers o' the Auld Crowd; ye'll pee yersel. And he's the only man I've heard sing in a doss for twenty year. Nae Pavarotti, but still his 'Midnight Special' was listenable. Likes the opera tae dis Erchie, foonder-member o' the Coatbridge Wagner Society; the only member. And a guid safe climber. Got me up the Trident on the Ben this year. Been oot a puckle times wi him.

Mind I telt ye aboot the time we met – we'll cry them the Cairn Toul Club – in the C.I.C. Hut? Aye, ye mind fine! Erchie hid nivver seen onything like it. It was like a hunner-year throw back. Octogenerian lawyers gyan tae bed wi the silk Paisley pattren pyjamas on; men o' the cloth reading their colloquial – **colloquial**, mind ye! – Serbo-Croat Grammars afore pittin oot their pipes. Ane o' them askit Erchie, fan he fund oot he'd graduated fae the steel works tae the squeel classroom, fit he taught, an near couped his tea at the reply; "Arseholes!" said Erchie.

We wis trying tae finish a' wir drink and food, afore gyan doon the next day, so we maun hae been a bit rowdy. Erchie ate athing, even a cole-slaw that wis hummin. Hummin, it wis singin looder nor Pavarotti! Next morning the mist wis richt doon. The Club were gettin happit up for their big day. The leader took charge; ilka member o' the party was gien a sling and a karabiner each. God kens fit they were tae dae wi that. Ootside, as we were getting ready, the leader cam up tae us peering through the horn-rimmed specs at the mirk that hung richt doon, and spiered, "Before you depart, gentlemen, could you be so kind as to direct us to Tower Ridge?"

It's the only time I've seen Erchie stung for words.

He pynted vaguely in the direction o' the Ben and we watched them depart single file. Then he recovered.

North Face Route

"Quick, let's get doon afore the Rescue passes us on the wye up, and ropes us in!"

But tae get back tae the story aboot Erchie at the reunion. Onywye, he got Davie worriet. Telt him the Creag Dhu were ca'in him 'The Spycatcher' for writing aboot them and spiering the identity o' the character the Big Yin, the ane that missed the deer on the poachin. Pit a few mair wrinkles on Davy's pow. Next day on the wye oot Erchie's fou in the morning, staggerin alang the road wi a can in ilka hand. So somebiddy gets ane back on him, pynts tae the cans, "That for balance, Erchie?"

And Davie wis a wee bit worriet next time we were headin past Jacksonville tae the Buachaille; fancied crossin the river a bit doonstream, oot o' sicht, in case he wis lynched. But we were seen crossin and had tae ging in. There wis Erchie again in his Gabby Hayes underwear, fryin up a cholesterol breakfast. It wis aboot 80 degrees ootside. And a few mair, including Big Maclean. Davie maun hae felt a bit like Bonington in '62. But there wis pleasant banter this time.

"I hear ye've written a book Davie, and I'm no in it," said ane. Asked foo sales were gyan.

"Fine. And I'm keepin ye for the next wan," came back Davie.

A wee bit crack and we were on oor wye. Relieved tae be alive Davie shot like a young thing up North Face Route and wisnae even grumpy fan, seconding, I couldnae get ane o' his runners oot and left it. Lunch on Heather Ledge in the sun, then up the crummlin chinmey past the rustet peg and, tae finish the day, danglin aff the variation finish wi a thoosand feet alow yer doup. A great day. No, we didnae bide the nicht there wi them. The 'Ville wis empty on the wye back. Davie mused tae himsel, "That scene this morning could hae been twenty year ago."

We went doon tae sweem at the Coupal Bridge in the big pool. That day the river had been kind, allowed us tae cross dry shod and gaen us a sweem. That day it hidnae shown us its black hairt.

Watter cannae ging aneath the same brig twice.

The Auld Crowd

I had not seen him for a long time; indeed I did not really know him all that well – some weekends down the years, some Creag Dhu dances. That was about the extent of it. Yet it came as a shock to hear that he was dead. You see, although Postie – as he was known – was one of the older members of the Auld Crowd (he must have been in his seventies) he looked much younger and was possessed of a spirit of restless energy which belied his years. He was the kind of guy you expected to go on for ever. But he was dead and that was an end to it.

Or was it? "You've missed the cremation." My informant hunched his shoulders against the cold and windy Glasgow street and looked glum. "But they're going to have a 'Do' for him up at Milarrochy Bay on Loch Lomondside. They're goin tae scatter his ashes roon the big fire. Leave him in a place he liked – wi people daen the kind of things he liked to do."

Milarrochy Bay, once a place of celebration for the Auld Crowd was now becoming their burial ground. I felt I wanted to go. I wanted to see the Auld Crowd and pay my last respects to one of their number. They are unique and their passing should be noted.

The Auld Crowd and the big fire. Images that have been with me most of my climbing life. The big fire at Craigallian Loch was the symbol of the beginning. The young men of the depression-sunk Clydeside who formed the vanguard of what has been called the 'proletarian revolution' in Scottish mountaineering, travelled there by the only means allowed by their poverty – they walked. Some came from Maryhill by way of Milngavie. Others left Clydebank and walked across the Old Kilpatrick Hills, passing the Whangie before dropping down to the valley of Carbeth above Strathblane. And at the loch they lit a fire; a fire that they said never went out, for there was always someone there. Equipment was basic – a Rodine can for a communual tea drum – blankets for some, old newspapers for others. But there they stayed and there they lifted their eyes to the blue mountains on the horizon. There they dreamt their dreams of distant peaks, and there they formed their clubs – the Lomonds, the Ptarmigan, and the Creag Dhu.

From this elemental beginning the proleterian exploration of the West of Scotland proceeded in a series of waves, dictated by the forms of transport and time available. Many who worked did so till late on a Saturday, so a quick dash to the bus for the Trossachs, or for Arrochar and the Cobbler had to suffice. Later, when organisation improved, lorries provided transport for distant Glencoe. Nimlin, a leading light of the period tells how:

> Innocent-looking lorries would roll out of Glasgow crammed to the shutters with suffering climbers. There was a time when one such wagon came to stop on the tramlines of a busy street. The driver could not wake it up, but after some minutes it began to move in a series of jerks. Someone peered out between the tarpaulins and saw a group of tram drivers, conductors and policemen bursting their braces to get it clear of the lines. He signalled for silence, but a whisper came from a dim corner 'If the polis ask what's in the lorry, make a noise like sheep.' (SMCJ XXVII 1963)

In transport, as in so many other ways, the approach of these new working-class climbers, created out of their economic circumstances, contrasted with that of their middle-class predecessors and contemporaries. Compare the above with what Murray, writing during the same pre-war period, said about cars.

> The new road to Glen Coe opened in 1935. Second-hand cars were cheap. I paid £8 for a 500cc Norton, which achieved 80 m.p.h. across the Moor of Rannoch. One snowy winter cured me of that. Thereafter it was saloon cars only. For £30 I bought an oil-eating Morris Minor that ran like a Rolls Royce until the door handles fell off. At such prices one could afford to climb. (SMCJ XXX 1975).

Small wonder, after years of watching from the deep freeze of desolate hitching spots, the affluent Scottish Mountaineering Club motor their comfortable way north, Creag Dhu members changed the shortened name of the SMC to the SMTC; the Scottish Motor Transport Club.

Economic differences also created different outlooks in areas divorced from the hills. Thus while we have no hint from the writings of Murray and others as to what their politics were (that is with the exception of J.H.B. Bell whose socialist views got him into trouble in the paper industry where he worked), many of this new breed were unashamedly socialist. This operated at a number of levels; at its simplest it was an emphasis on group loyalty and group solidarity, combined with a hostility to the lairds and their attempts to keep the land to themselves and their deer. Consequently there was scant regard paid to pleas to stay off the hill during the stalking season. At its most lofty it was fighting, and sometimes dying, for the Republican cause in the Spanish Civil War. Postie at the age of fourteen travelled to the recruiting centre in Paris only to be turned away because of his youth.

Finally, whereas Murray admitted to preferring hotels in the winter, the working-class mountaineers sought out, in all seasons, the cheapest form of accommodation; that which costs nothing, the howff and the bothy. It could have been the caves in Glen Loin at Arrochar, or under the boulders high up in the Cobbler Corrie. At the Trossachs you would have found them under the inadequate boulder at Tinker's Loan. Sometimes they made their own howffs as in Glencoe when they threw an old tarpaulin over the corner of a sheep fank on the site of what is now known as Jacksonville. At other times they just slept out under a 'tarp' slung between the trees as at Tyndrum – a practice still carried out today. 'Tarps' used to be buried at a number of different sites all over the Highlands. They provided an unexpected source of food for the local mice population whose nibbled holes led to much discomfort for the human users on rainy nights. More ease was to be found in the newly-emptied outlying estate cottages, the casual occupation of which led to the unique bothying tradition of Scottish mountaineering.

Of course the going was hard. A youthful Jimmy Marshall recalls

an earlier and more primitive version of Jacksonville, the spiritual, as
well as physical, home of the Creag Dhu, as 'a stygian hollow' a bit
too close to the river for comfort.

> High water came and went, leaving us in its aftermath, perched
> on narrow planks, sorting ourselves out in a fastidious attempt to
> avoid contact with an unspeakable mire, masquerading as a floor.
> (SMCJ XXXIII 1984).

And from the deep recesses of my memory come scraps of half
remembered songs of a contemporary bard. Songs that immortalised
not only the dosses but gave some indication of the difficulties, self
inflicted or otherwise experienced by the occupants:

> Cold winter was howling o're moor and o're mountain
> When out of the Baillie a climber was thrown
> As he lay in the gutter
> I heard some one mutter
> He's stinkin of booze that is not his own
>
> Hey ho Lovat lie easy
> Your own grave will never be known
> But by the lord Jesus
> This winter will freeze us
> We'll die in the doss they call Tinker's Loan

Another song recalls a doss, now long gone, at Croftamie:–

> In fields and the hills of Croftamie
> Where young men fear to tread
> There's a long winding track
> That leads to a shack
> In the land of the so-called dead
>
> If you peer through the grime on the windows
> You will see on each bunk
> A wine-sodden drunk
> Who hikes for the good of his health.

This was the background of the men I knew as the Auld Crowd.
Some, like the Purvis brothers, following in the footsteps of the

previous generation, started their career simply by walking out of Glasgow. They met other like-minded people who told them of other good hills, bothies and howffs and thus began a career which was to last a lifetime. Others were old Creag Dhuers. Indeed the Auld Crowd seems to have been a refuge for older members whose powers had failed, or for whom the slippery verticals had lost their attractions.

One or two, a long time ago in their wild young days, took the odd beast from the hill. Nothing commercial it should be understood – just the odd one for the pot. Some of the deer were so old they practically gave themselves up. Some were not so obliging.

Some men had been correcting the sight of the rifle by firing at a tin can. Eventually the tin can was hit giving rise to the expectation that if the rifle was pointed in the direction of a deer success was to be assured. That this proved not to be the case led to a rise of general scepticism in the assembled company. At length, after some abortive dispersion of lead, one laconic wit reduced the party to tears. "Perhaps if you put a tin can on wan o' their heids you would be able to shoot it."

Although consisting of non-climbers and retired climbers, the influence of the Auld Crowd on my generation cannot be over-exaggerated. What they gave to us was the concept of weekending. Basically this was an all-round approach to the weekly escape from the world of work. Unlike today when there are so many who go Munro-bagging on a Sunday, or who single-mindedly pursue the ever-rising high standards of modern rock-climbing, these men took a wider interest in matters concerning the hills. They took pride in being out in all weathers, making themselves comfortable and enjoying the music and stories of their fellows. The fire was a central element in all this – a meeting place, as well as a source of comfort. They would even build a fire during a short wait for someone who was giving them a lift. Rain and wet wood were not an excuse for failing in these endeavours, for it used to be said that they could light one using wet confetti for tinder.

For the Auld Crowd reputations made in climbing meant nothing. What became important was that you were there to take part – to go on the hill and in the evening to listen or to tell the stories, and join in the 'crack'. Thus for the remnants of the Auld Crowd going away today has as much significance as it did in their youth. As one confided to me recently "Ah'm never so completely happy as when Ah'm away the weekend." And for this kind of happiness some are willing to travel several thousand miles a year. One member of the Auld Crowd forced, like so many Scots, to seek a decent standard of living abroad, flies back from Canada several times a year to 'weekend'. Others have been known to come back from New Zealand.

Another important and long standing aspect of the Auld Crowd which influenced us, is their loyalty to one another. Thus even when severely incapacitated, as is Jim Purvis with Multiple Sclerosis, he is not forgotten or left behind. A lot of consideration and effort goes into making sure he gets away as many weekends as is practical. Indeed recently a helicopter flight was organised for Jim which took in all his old haunts such as Loch Lomondside, Beinn Dorain and the Rannoch Moor, before landing briefly at Ben Alder cottage, a favourite bothy. As Hector, one of the passengers, pointed out. "Fifty years of 'weekending' in an hour".

These were some of the thoughts that ran through my head as I drove up by Drymen and on to Balmaha. And at Milarrochy Bay there they were. Hector, a prince among men, welcoming as ever, cutting large logs for the huge fire; Sardines, guitar at the ready for the inevitable singing and many others: the Purvis brothers, wee Onnie McGill and his brother. Later, other older fellows whom I did not know were to emerge from out of the bushes as if they had walked up from Balmaha. They were welcomed into the company and large glasses of whisky were thrust into their hands. Food too was available, for round the big fire some of the lads were frying square sausages, a favourite repast, in large black frying pans. It occurred to me then that you can always tell a 'weekender' by his cooking equipment, for though clean on the inside it is black on the outside with woodsmoke and tar.

Eventually the company was called to gather round the big fire where one man spoke a magnificent eulogy in memory of Postie. We heard of his beginnings – 'one of the first of the working-class mountaineers' – his energy, companionship and generosity. This done the ashes, in somber mood and with dignity, were scattered around the fire and down into the Loch itself.

While the ceremony was proceeding I noticed that we were being observed by two very different groups. The first of these was on the loch itself. Clad in their brightly-coloured wet-suits, and hanging on to their strange craft, the wind-surfers drifted by on the lightest of breezes, looking in silent amazement at the motley crew and their doings on shore. There could be no more elegant statement of the passing of the old world and the coming of the new. The former, forged in a poverty now long gone, spoke of simple practicalities – the utilitarian clothes, the comradeship of years on the hills – cloaking complex values. The latter told of complex superficialities. A world of style without substance; the gold bars on the virile chest, the Ford Sierra on the shore. Thus while the old merged with the territory (a product of long-gone poaching days) the new screamed look at me! They were certainly different cultures – they could have been from different planets.

The other group of observers were from the same planet, but they were rather like anthropologists who have stumbled upon a hitherto unknown exotic tribe. They had been 'doing' the West Highland Way when they chanced upon our clearing. There, arrested by the sights and sounds of the ceremony, they stood quietly for some minutes, giving us a chance to take their measure. They were new to the hiking game; their wee woolly hats, their badly-packed gear, the redness of their faces, and their heavy breathing from gaping mouths marked their poor state of fitness, inexperience and naivety.

Someone detached himself from our mourning group, simultaneously hushing and welcoming the interlopers with glasses of whisky. But the newcomers could not be contained and soon had their cameras out to photograph us from all directions. I knew then how third-world peasants felt when confronted with pack of vociferous tourists. Someone tried to explain to them the significance of these events but though they nodded their heads in understanding their faces were blank with incomprehension. I could only hope that their journey would help fill in the spaces, for that is what such journeys are for. Perhaps, then, my intolerance is unforgivable for we all must start somewhere. To see and to understand will require many journeys and the experience gained will make us.

Later, when I left to drive back to Glasgow, I could not but think of other haunts of the Auld Crowd. Especially memorable was the bar behind the Royal Hotel, Tyndrum. It was an exceedingly small, narrow and bare place, decorated only by two glass cases. The first of these contained three stuffed trout, the significance of which was never apparent to me – they looked so ordinary! In contrast to these tiddlers the second, larger case, which was fixed above the bar, contained a huge stuffed carcase of a rather disagreeable-looking salmon which had been killed (not caught, mark you) in the River Orchy.

Packed, as it was in the summer with hordes of thirsty tourists, it was a rather uncomfortable bar to patronise. But in winter during the early 60s, before the traffic created by the skiing, and when only a handful of hardy mountaineers were on the road competing for lifts from the thin traffic, it became a place transformed. Then, on many a cold Sunday night, you would find the Auld Crowd delaying the moment when they would have to return to Glasgow, Monday and work.

Filtered through the years come back memories of Wee Onnie standing on the table his glass raised, his head thrown back to sing 'The Bar Room Mountaineers', while some other character, a navvy from the Cruachan Dam complete with a Rangers' muffler round his neck, danced a jig on the bar, his head bouncing off the light. And there was Findlay, the barman who always had a welcoming word, clapping his hands in wondrous appreciation. For company there would be some of the locals. Old Strachan who lived in a caravan in Glen Orchy, and who always claimed there was gold in the hills above Coninish long before it was found by the mining company. Or Tex who seemed to live in one of the railway bothies. There never was a bar like Findlay's at Tyndrum! Sadly, Tyndrum is no place for a bar which caters for a small, old and dying trade.

Findlay's has gone along with the man who gave his name to it. Another milestone in the passing of an age, Findlay died last year.

By the time I got to Drymen it was raining and as I passed the Buchanan Arms, another favourite meeting place of the Auld Crowd, I began to think of all the personalities of which it consisted. Every member was a character in his own right, but of all the characters in the Auld Crowd there is one who stands out and deserves special mention. When I first met Hector he was a semi-professional wrestler, who, because of his superb Latin American moustache, used to fight under a Mexican name. Hence, despite his solid Glasgow origins, his arrival at the ring would be heralded by the throbbing music of Spanish guitars and shouts of loud olé's. His costume of large sombrero and poncho would complete the disguise.

My first meeting with Hector was as bizarre as the man. We were hitch-hiking at Tarbert, Loch Lomond, Todd and I. And a strange pair of hitchers we were. Well, I was all right. It was Todd who looked a bit odd, for along with the normal accoutrements of the weekend, he held in one hand – in much the same way a knight would hold a lance – a collapsible film projection screen. In the other hand he held the accompanying slide-projector. The purpose of these objects, and why we came to be stranded at Tarbet that night, is a long story that need not concern the reader. Suffice it to say that Todd's car, in which we had been travelling, was installed in the garage of that village, looking sad after a confrontation with a large boulder which for some malevolent reason had placed itself in the middle of the road.

We had been there some little time, failing to impress anyone of our need for transportation, when a small van came hurtling round the corner, its tyres squealing. It rushed towards us and then stopped with a distinct smell of burning rubber. Inside and behind the wheel was Hector, slightly over-refreshed. How we got to Tyndrum I shall never know. The road, much more primitive than today's smooth highway, offered more than a few opportunities for us to dash ourselves down some steep embankment, or against some pitiless tree. However even the horrendous double bend which used to grace the old railway bridge at Glen Falloch failed to interrupt our furious progress, despite the fact that we seemed to go round it sideways. Thus for Todd and I, arrival was gratefully achieved. As for Hector, he seemed oblivious to the consternation he had caused. He was in the bar doing what he was famous for: cracking jokes and creating his marvellously spontaneous fun.

In the years that followed I was to see a lot of Hector and enjoy his brand of anarchic humour. One incident which will give some indication of the genius of the man stands out in my mind. It was a Creag Dhu social weekend somewhere in the Highlands. The club and their friends had dined and had retired to the bar where Hector was entertaining everyone with a series of improvised jokes. Everyone, that is, except the barman. For some reason he had taken a dislike to Hector. "Anymore o' that daft patter and you're out pal." He threatened. Hector, who was standing against the bar, was not intimidated by this and continued with his repartee.

"That's it," the barman exploded. "You're for it now pal." And he whipped off the glasses which he wore, laid them down on the bar and began to march round, rolling up his sleeves as he went in order to do battle. Hector looking shocked, turned round to lay the upper half of his body on the bar and covered his head with his hands as if terrified of the approaching barman. "Aw naw," he cried. "Doe-ent, doe-ent!"

At this point a number of people, remembering Hector's prodigious feats in the wrestling ring moved in to form a barrier around Hector. There were cries of. "For goodness sake don't hit him Hecky!"

Undeterred, the barman came on, pushing his way through the crowd which surrounded the prone body of Hector. On reaching him the barman leaned over, caught him by the shoulders and as he lifted him from the bar he spun him around. There was a gasp from the crowd. The barman stood transfixed. Hector was wearing the barman's glasses. "You wouldnae hit a man wi glasses on, would ye?", he asked innocently as the crowd collapsed in laughter.

It was at this point that the manager of the hotel arrived. He ordered the combatative but now deflated barman back to his station, and then walked with a distinct limp to join Hector. "They

tell me Hector, that you're a bit of a wrestler. Is that true?" he asked
as he leant his elbow on the bar. Hector did not answer, but with
swift professional movements seized the manager's leg. This time it
was Hector's turn to stop in amazement for the leg in his hands
stuck out from the manager's body at a strange and unnatural angle.
Once again the onlookers gasped. Hector looked up at the manager
and smiled. "Have you got a wooden leg?" The manager nodded
and the crowd again collapsed in laughter.

Hector was at the centre of many wild weekends. There was
McGarva's weekend at Inversnaid to celebrate his forthcoming
marriage. Beside 'This darksome burn, horseback brown' we did
cavort. We slept out on the shore to be 'degged with dew, dappled
with dew'. And we were wet and wild, though not in the way
expressed by Gerard Manley Hopkins who wrote this famous poem,
Inversnaid. For behaviour we thought mild – just the usual singing,
excluding the rude songs – we were barred from the hotel.
Afterwards, as we came out into the warm afternoon sun, Hector
stripped off his clothes and ran to dive from the pier into the Loch.
An act of sheer exuberance; his celebration of life.

This diving was to be repeated in the culmination of the weekend.
We were sailing back to Balloch on the old, now sadly defunct,
paddle steamer, the 'Maid of the Loch' and as usual the Auld Crowd
had taken it over. Some were crowded into the bar where a singing
session was taking place. Others gave an impromptu concert using
the platform above one of the paddles. The tourists seemed
delighted to be entertained in a way not mentioned in the brochures.
Even the captain, standing on the open bridge, smiled, sometimes in
nervous apprehension, sometimes in appreciation.

Then as we rounded the headland that greeted our arrival at
Rowardennan, something very strange happened. One of the Auld
Crowd, a wee bit refreshed, mistook the pier for Balloch. He began
to take off his clothes, all the while muttering about not having a
ticket and how he would have to dive off the boat to avoid paying.
The boat was swinging into the pier when our fare dodger, stripped
to his underpants, climbed onto the balustrade just to the left of the
paddles, there to balance awaiting the optimum moment for his dive;

a considerable feat in view of his state of inebriation. The boat approached the pier. The diver swayed atop the balustrade. The singing and the jokes petered out; surely he was not going to dive down into certain death. Still the boat came on, and still he hovered, balancing forwards and then backwards to counteract the movements of the boat. The resolution of this desperate situation came when the boat nudged the pier and the diver fell backwards, disappearing from sight noisily and painfully down a circular steel stairway. The onlookers held their collective breath. He must be hurt yet no one moved. Then after what seemed an age, a head appeared, face fixed in a silly grin. The infamous relaxation of drunks had saved him. Relieved, someone cracked, "You're sum diver, you'ur. This loch's twenty miles long and six miles wide and you missed it!"

Time, as it must, has caught up with the Auld Crowd. Some are dead and others' health is such that they can no longer go away weekending. But there is still a remnant who do not allow their infirmities to diminish their ability to 'weekend'. The following brief tale is an illustration of the tenacity of men who have never forgotten the importance of getting out into the hills.

They had a difficult time getting to that spot. The boat was overloaded with food, gear and of course, a wee refreshment. Some of the boatmen were a wee bit over refreshed. The consequence, if it was indeed a consequence, for such events can happen when all are sober, was a capsize. Purvis suffering from Multiple Sclerosis had to be rescued quickly. Another was saved by his colostomy bag keeping him up as he floated away. Later Hector, suitably weighed down with stones tied to his legs, had to dive to rescue the drink from its watery resting place. Morale was thus restored and everyone enjoyed themselves.

You may have come across them in some bar on the road to the north. To your modern eye they may have been dismissed as a noisy anachronism. However you would be wrong. They are a product of their times and their culture. Their solution to the dreariness of work or unemployment; to the powerlessness and poverty; to the overcrowded tenement and crumbling backcourt, was to take to the

The Auld Crowd, Young

road and the hills. In doing so they built their own unique lifestyle
and value system. It came from deep inside them; a part of their
natural and real existence. Thus it was not some passing fashion, but
something that was to endure a lifetime. Of course there was a price
to pay and some might ask about the wives and children left behind
while they spent time in their exclusively male world. This was not
unusual and in this they were no different from others of their
generation. And yet they were different because when most men
sought their solution to life in the pub and betting shop, they got out
into the hills. They came to know that there was something other
than the city and that there was a world of freedom beyond the gates
of the factory.

Their symbol was 'the fire' and for Postie his life was a journey
between two fires – Craigallian and Milarrochy Bay. His death
marked the beginning of the passing of an age. So if you are lucky
enough to come across the Auld Crowd, take note for they are the
last of the true proletarian mountaineers. The conditions that
created them have passed into history, and you will never see their
likes again.

> What would the world be, once bereft
> Of wet and of wildness? Let them be left,
> O let them be left, wildness and wet;
> Long live the weeds and the wilderness yet.
> (Gerard Manley Hopkins *Inversnaid*).

Second Ascent, Variation

He had been there twice before. The first time in his mother's womb, the second carried in her arms. Both times his father had been there. Now he walked unaided beside that father in the full power of his almost five years. Refusing all aid, with his eyes he searched for the top where lay the promised hill-fort. Scrambling towards the summit cairn through and beyond the walls, crumbled, of the vitrified rampart, his query raised smiles from the couple sitting by the path. "Will the Picts still be at the top?" His father caught up with him, lifted him up and seated him on the cairn, from where he could see the countryside stretching from the North Sea inland by wood and field to the Cairngorms white on the horizon. "Na, loon. The Picts are lang gane. And the Romans as weel." "Why did the Romans try and kill the Picts? That was nasty." "Greed for gear, loon, They cam tae see if there was onything worth takkin. But there wasnae so they went haim. Look at yon hill wi the snaw. That's Lochnagar, far yer faither started climbing." Again, a finger pointed at a distraction and verbal trickery managed to stem briefly the torrent of unanswerable questions. The boy ran about the summit by the short cliff describing what he would do to the Romans if they came again. Meanwhile his father looked from Bennachie towards Lochnagar.

> Bennachie; Far the Gadie rins.
>
> Oh, gin I were far the Gadie rins,
> the Gadie rins, the Gadie rins,
> Oh, gin I were far the Gadie rins,
> At the back o' Bennachie
>
> I waud ne'er come back again,
> back again, back again,
> I waud ne'er come back again,
> Ye Lowland lads tae see.

His father had sung the boy this song nightly for most of his short life. The result had been the boy's developing obsession with the mountain which formed into an absolute insistence that it be climbed this holiday. The mountain dominates the rolling country-side of Aberdeenshire, its coned summit and hump-backed torso visible from almost anywhere in the North-east, attracting the eye. Forest gives way to moor and then to rock on this miniature Matterhorn of the Garioch. Though it was already April, powder-snow had fallen on the hill two days before.

The day started at Esson's Croft. His father took him to the ruins of the houses of the land raiders who had squatted on the commonty till driven off by the lairds. "Why did they not take away the laird's land?" His father paused, looking for the sentence that would be no lie but would curtail the discussion. "False consciousness, loon, and an objectively bad situation for the class-struggle. But come on, lace up yer beets and we'll get gyan. We've a muckle hill tae climb, bynear as high as Ben Nevis." His energy came in waves, headlong rushes, followed by states of near-collapse. These crises were overcome by cajolery, distractions and half-way up, by food and drink. After the trees thinned out and the summit became visible there was no doubt that he would make it. Nothing would have stopped him.

His father's own first experience of the hill had not been so successful. He had been ten years old and was with the para-military Boy's Brigade when an incompetent leader had dragged them through thick forest which defeated the entire party. Many years later he became a regular visitor to its tops; the first time not even noticing the fort, the second wondering what it was, knowing on the third. But now his son had gained the top and breached the fort's defenses at a first attempt.

"Have you climbed Bennachie before, Daddy?" His father looked down at the questioner. "Aye loon, many times. I was here wi yer mither and ane or two afore her. And I was here wi Stumpy, Cuddy and mair, plotting hoo tae get rid o' the lairds and the like. Ye see doon there? That's far the battle o' Harlaw was focht." He pointed North-eastwards to Inverurie and the small eyes followed. *Harlaw*:

another song he had sung, aiming to induce sleep but not that only. Also a knowledge of a tongue that was dying even here in its heartland and which he knew the boy would never hear in Glasgow where he was growing up. His father had heard the great Jeanie Robertson sing the epic ballad ending with,

> Sic a weary burying
> I'm sure ye nivver saw
> As was on the Sunday aifter that
> On the muir aneath Harlaw
>
> Gin onybody spier at ye
> For them that's gaen awa
> Tell their wives and bairnies
> They're sleeping at Harlaw

"What was MacDonald fighting for at Harlaw?" "He wanted tae be King but there was ane a'ready and the Lowlanders wanted that ane." "Would it have been good if MacDonald had won?" He smiled: the Highland sympathies of the boy's mother. "Weel loon, at that time it was historically progressive for MacDonald tae get beat. Look doon there, that's Balquain Castle." A ruin when his father was a boy, it was now restored as a private residence. From there seven sons had set out to go to Harlaw with their father. Their mother cried, 'Spare me the runtie' and kept the youngest back, the only one to survive. The man looked down at his own runtie, following what he could of his father's antiquarian commentary on the landscape. An audience that never tired of it, an audience at last.

....

Other songs the man had sung the boy who thought his father the supreme singer till he discovered on a commercial tape Fishgut Mac, a friend of his father's youth and the latter was relegated to only occasional songs. But this pleased rather than hurt him since Mac could not sing to his own daughter, born deaf. 'Ben Lomond' was such a song, leading to an obsession in the young mind on a par with that over Bennachie.

Repeated requests had worn down resistance. The father had been reading of the early men, of Naismith and Raeburn, but even

Ben Lomond Summit

their prodigious beginnings had taken place when they were much older than the four year old at his feet with his wee boots, tiny pack, and determination. A fine day had dawned and he was to be allowed to experience his first failure. A salutary lesson that would allow his skills to develop at a more leisured pace.

A mountain for the unfit, the elderly, parents and their children (but none so young). A mere half hour out of Glasgow a path leads direct to the top; but still a full 3,000 ft. of ascent is involved. His father had been here several times with novitiates and from its top the lands that now rivalled in affection those seen from the top of Bennachie stretched away.

The boy started like the wind, his parents unable to keep up. But by the time the stile to the moor was reached he was puggled, wabbit. On the open moor facing the cold wind, the heavy mud, seeing the distance, he flagged and had to be cajoled. At the ridge leading to the summit a squall blew up. His father held the small hands in his own to warm them and spoke encouragement but the boy was failing. "Daddy, I don't think I can do it" "But we're nearly there. And look, there's the tap." Should he lift him, or go back down? Then the squall blew over as quickly as it had risen and a weak sun provided enough warmth and cheer to give encouragement for the last few hundred feet. On the summit he ran, again leaving his father behind despite a fall, to reach the summit cairn. "Did you not think I could do it?" he queried as his father approached. "I kent fine ye could, ance ye stopped greeting." But he could not take a step farther, up or down. After pointing out to the boy his future battlefields, the Cobbler, Ben Laoigh, Glencoe, they descended. He assumed the burden of paternity. Into his father's rucksack and onto his shoulders crawled the victor of the day to relive his long march to victory on the way down, in a stream of prattle. At one point a slip led to a minor fall which forced tears – as much of exhaustion as of pain. "That spoiled the day." "Na, son. Ye'll forget that wee dunt afore nicht. But ye'll remember this day a yer life. Yer first Munro." "Did a wee boy of four do a Munro before?" "I dinna ken, but I wouldnae nane think it." Back at the loch the sack was emptied of its burden.

Then there was his first bothy. From an early age the boy had been fascinated by the picture in the kitchen of his father drying a sock by a fire. Requests and pleadings again became so insistent that, again, his father gave in. The forecast of thirty-six hours dry weather opened a window of opportunity and so they headed for the bothy where the sock had been dried – in Glen Feshie.

Three previous days of lashing rain and fears over the weather added to his father's worry that the boy might not make the walk in. It was four miles from where they left the car. Starting off with a mini-pack of clothes and teddy bear the boy soon abandoned this burden to his father. A couple of crises were surmounted by sustenance and fantasy and finally after three and a bittock miles along the wooded riverside the bothy could be discerned through the trees. By now he was running, falling, and picking himself up in his ardour to be there. Then he stopped, allowing his father to catch up. "Daddy, Daddy, give me the sack, so that if anybody's there they'll think I carried it all the way." With a smile his father acquiesced in the subterfuge but he was the only one to witness the boy's triumph. The bothy was uncharacteristically empty. As his father watched, the son ran around the bothy, in and out of both rooms, up and downstairs by the wooden ladder, wordless. The fire – the one on the photograph – was lit and as the boy tended it with pine cones his father prepared him his first bothy meal. Exhausted, the boy was then carried upstairs to bed. But as his father sat below tending the fire, he could hear him talking to his bear above, for hours, about mountains and bothies. Below the man meditated on the previous times he'd tended the fire; with the boy's mother, with companions drinking round its flame. He took a seat to the door and watched the deer coming down to the river flats to graze in the evening and the hawks hanging over the rabbits nibbling on the hill thick with juniper behind the bothy. This the boy could see with his own eyes one day. If he wanted to.

....

And his first defeat did come before he was much older.

"Daddy, I want to go back." He said it instantly before his father made the decision to retreat, cursing himself for previous hesitation.

Fionn Bheinn; the easiest of hills. They started from the moor bending their way through a plantation athwart the path, irritated by the scratching pine needles. Then a faint stalkers' path overgrown to a mossy carpet, indistinct, eased the ascent. The sky was heavy but the top was clear. Lunch was in the lee of a stone dyke which led like an arrow to the summit ridge. The wind rose a little so they walked on the sheltered side, the boy not rising above the dyke but his babble rising above the wind. His father stilled it on the ascent by telling the boy to look: the Fannaichs, Torridon.

The dyke led them to the summit ridge but no further. It looked complete from below but had spilled stones down at several points where gusts of wind caught the boy. His father asked, "Foo wid ye get doon, if I broke my leg or something?" "I would follow the dyke."

Still it was easy, hardly drawing the breath of either till they were a few hundred feet below the summit where it steepened. The drizzle had started but the boy was well happit up, so that did not trouble him. He affirmed that he would, could, continue. Till the angle eased off and they lost the shelter of the slope, baring them to the force of the wind. It was not a gale but it snatched your breath and then thrust it back down your throat and upset the balance. The boy was troubled, his father could see. He was debating carrying him, back to the wind, and walking the few hundred feet to the summit when the boy spoke and made both their decisions. They began to walk back. "I'll hae tae come back tae yon daft hill, I've still nae done it!" the man informed the new leader. "Still, nae tae worry, it's been there a few million years, it'll bide there a puckle yet."

Down through the thickening mist, they stopped in the lee of a bank to take a compass bearing. "Are you lost, Daddy?" Piqued, he replied, "Na, na. We've jist come a wee bit far tae the north. If we climb back up yon bit, we'll get tae the dyke." And climb back they did. The dyke sheltered and led them down out of the mist. Descending they saw the deer, heads raised, questioning. At the burn they stopped to drink and watch the dragonflies' wings blue sheen over the water.

The boy had descended on his own this time, unaided, uncarried. Unmarked and untroubled. Unaware of the breaches in the dyke, yet.

They saw the deer, lying in twisted rigidity. It was beside the fallen fence around the plantation. His father had noticed the smell on the ascent but not noticed the body where it lay. The boy, ahead, was looking at it. When his father arrived at the scene he was asked, "What's the matter with the deer, Daddy?" "It's deid loon, that's fit." He eased the boy away over the fence and down through the wood. The boy walked easily underneath the branches that irritated his father and obscured his view. "Will I die, Daddy?" The boy had stopped in a brief clearing; his father stopped too, hesitant. The boy repeated the question. "Maybe they'll hae fun a cure, ere yer growd up. Maye ye'll nae dee," he offered. "But will they find a cure?" In the darkness of the wood there was no relief from the irritation of the needles. "Na, they'll nae find a cure, loon, there's nae remied." Taking his son's hand the father emerged from the wood and crossed the moor to the road.

....

He was wrenched from his musings by yet another question. "Where's Ben A'n?" His father smiled, moving his gaze from Lochnagar to the boy on the cairn. "Ye cannae see that fae here."

That had been the boy's first real ascent. Naked at three on a sweltering hot day, he had run to the top passing the rocks where Clydeside climbers of several generations had trained. His father pointed out Ash Tree Wall and noted that he had climbed it. But the boy was only interested in gaining the top. From there they saw the steamer on the loch and he promised the boy a sail in it after descent. On the way down his father referred to the rocks again and this time elicited more interest. "Who looks after you, Daddy, when you're climbing?" "Davie looks after me loon, dinna worry." On board the boat the relentless questioning continued. Watching his father buy tickets he asked, "Do you have to pay for everything?" "Aye, loon. That's the market economy. Generalised commodity relations." "You shouldn't have to pay, you shouldn't!" the child insisted. "There's lots o' folk have said that. But let's see if the engines rin on coal or ayl".

Given a moment's peace his father again surveyed the Cairngorm horizon. After Bennachie there had been a school trip to Beinn a' Bhuird. The teacher had been a fool who led a party of kids twenty miles over the mountain, screaming at stragglers. When they met a group of youths with tents and rucksacks the teacher commented deprecatingly to his charges in gym shoes, clutching lemonade bottles, "They're real mountaineers, now." That had been another false start and shortly afterwards he had been immobilised by an accident for two years. But soon he could outwalk all but the strongest; at a price he was willing to pay.

His boy's path would be easier. Following in his footsteps but without the mistakes and false turnings. Doing it again and getting it right. Every man thinks his son is the Redeemer, correcting his own sins or omissions.

He had fled from the boy before and after his birth; a birth he had not, or rather a conception he had not, planned. He tried to forget its incipience in a massive bout of mountaineering. He had accomplished with ease walks which before had been beyond his faulted powers. The Mamores fell in a day, he nearly died battling through a snowdrift to the bothy at Bruar. He ran away, each time to return, surprised, to find the child still there. Climbing he took up again after many, many years, as if somehow to escape, bridge the chasm which was closing in on him. Only facing fear again, (he had never been a competent climber) was he able to relieve the obsession, lift the tightness that otherwise never left his chest. Even after birth, when the boy metamorphosed from a threat to a reality, his father fled from him, held him at arm's length, tried to suppress his feelings for, about, him.

It was on the Skye Cuillin. The boy was three months old and again his progenitor had run away, to attempt the traverse of the Cuillin ridge. The attempt failed (they lost their water and in a state of collapse from dehydration descended after Sgurr a' Mhadaidh with only three of eleven peaks remaining) – and so too failed his attempted flight from his son. Moving up from Glen Brittle in an evening of heavy air and sky, mist low on the mountains, they encountered a light rain. At Coire nan Laogh they were forced high to escape the clouds of midgies pursuing them like furies as the sweat poured out of their bodies. Finally an uplift breeze floated into the corrie and took away the mist and the tormentors. His companion stretched a survival bag over a rock and they lay underneath for a few hours' uneasy rest before the dawn. The sheet was shorter than his body. His face was uncovered and on it a light rain started to fall. He lay with his eyes open looking towards Sgurr nan Eag and gave up the struggle. His son was the alternative range of possibilities to those his birth had closed off; a new belay for his father's life.

....

They descended from Bennachie. He noticed the boy stepping into his adult footsteps on the muddy path. "Gang yer ain gate, loon. Dinna follae in my dubs!" And he knew himself the boy would soon tire of matching his stride to his father's. Knew he could live for the boy but the boy would not live for him.

Requiem for Willie

For years I had never gone near that part of the city. Then, because of a number of those trivial events of which mundane lives are made, I found myself travelling by that way on a number of occasions. Each time I passed the tenement I would draw myself forward in my seat to get a better view of it, and I would think of Willie.

The tenement on Springburn Road still stands. It is lucky, for little else on Springburn Road still stands. It used to be such a busy place. The tenements with the pubs and shops below, people teeming in the streets, the huge railway works where Willie's dad worked. Gone, all gone; replaced by a new road to help the commuters and shoppers get from leafy Bishopbriggs to town a little faster. What is left of the population swept up into a complex of tower blocks. While there is little point in being sentimental about the widespread demolition of what could appear, on a foggy Glasgow night, to be a dismal place to live, the people of Springburn deserved better than this.

Yet the tenement still stands. Between the old cemetery and the new dual carriageway, raised above the main road, its ancient street buttressed by wooden shores against some impending disaster. It is one of the few enduring tenements and it has been renovated. Its blunt southern snout cleaned for the first time since its construction. Its windows have been replaced. When I pass I especially look at the window of the room where the coffin lay. The last time I passed, that window was open and someone, a stranger, was looking out, his arms crossed, his elbows resting on the sill.

Let me see; when did all this happen? Something like thirty years ago, was it not? I wonder if there are still neighbours about to tell the new people about the coffin? Would they even think to talk of it? Yet that is the kind of thing people think about when they come to a new home, is it not? The folk who lived there before them. Their lives,

157

Tenement

and their deaths. It was in that room with the bed recess. I remember
it well. The room darkened by the curtains drawn in respect for the
dead. The coffin, standing on its trestles to one side near that
window, had its lid screwed down. The room was stuffy, crowded as
it was with friends and family. My young head was reeling from the
early morning whiskies dispensed by Willie's brave father to fortify
the mourners. My knees were bending as the crush of people
pushed me against the bed. So instead of mourning Willie, I spent
those solemn moments struggling to prevent myself falling backwards into the recessed bed. He was dead; his head crushed by that
fall and all I was worried about was maintaining my contact with the
room.

Willie's death made him famous. The accident was reported on
the front page of the *Sunday Post*. I wonder if there are still
neighbours about who could tell of that day when the large crowd
gathered around the close entrance to watch the coffin being
manhandled as elegantly as the steep stairs and narrow close would
allow? The crowd surged forward as we, Willie's friends, left.
"There they are," people cried. "Those are the ones who cause
their parents so much pain!" They touched, pushed us even;
crowded around us with such a pressure that we were glad to get into
the limousine, there to light up our cigarettes. I was numb. Not, if I
remember correctly, with grief, but with shock. The young cannot
grieve for the dead for what does death mean to them? Their youth
and their belief in their own immortality protects them from the grief
which afflicts their elders.

This numbness may account for the little I remember of what
happened at the crematorium. Only fragments remain. Some
minister going on about understanding climbing as a method of
getting closer to God. But did we realise the anguish to which we
subjected our parents? He was not on Willie's side. Then to the
accompaniment of the low rumbling, humming sound of the furnace
that the discreet organ music can never hide, the coffin sank slowly
beneath its blue cover.

Later, much subdued, we regrouped at the Red Lion. We had
attended the refreshments back at the house on Springburn Road,

drunk some more whisky, eaten the sandwiches and talked to Willie's relatives. However we were drawn, as always, back to our favourite place in the town; the Red Lion on West Nile Street where we used to meet to plan our weekends. We loved the beer and the strangely mixed clientele. The crooks who ran the protection rackets, the hard-drinking shipyard workers who used it as a town base, the posing drama students from the Athenaeum round the corner. To buy a drink was a performance for them. I, really just out of school and escaping for the first time from dreary suburbia, felt so grown up and sophisticated to be there – a part of Glasgow town life. I drank in the atmosphere. There were, occasionally, brief sharp fights and one night some guy got knocked through the bamboo partition that separated the two main booths. The Red Lion has gone now. Replaced first by one of those formica palaces which brewers in the 1970s seemed to think their customers would appreciate. Now, several failed refurbishments later on, it has one of those daft names people think are trendy. 'Braces' or 'Flies', or some such thing. No doubt it will soon be a wine bar.

Anyway, we had a few drinks and then things went downhill rapidly. A meal in a Chinese restaurant ended with us taking a 'runner' pursued by irate waiters. We lost them in the old Cowcaddens: that confusion of rotten black tenements which used to be found to the north of the city centre. They too have disappeared. It was when we stopped to catch our breath that Joe decided to relieve himself up a close. As he stood swaying slightly, steam issuing forth from the region of his feet, a door in the close opened and out stepped an irate occupant to remonstrate with him. There was much shouting and pushing as Joe was urged to the close mouth, still clutching his member which dripped disconsolately onto his shoes. We joined in the scuffling but it did not come to much. Just some ritualistic verbal challenges before the two sides separated, the man to his flat, and we, the mourners now dishevelled, black ties askew, shirt tails hanging out, dusty and tired with that peculiar afternoon hangover, to our homeward journeys. The last echoing voice died in the worn street. "Getawayyamugye". Yes, our grieving was flawed.

Some time later we carried Willie's ashes up to the Waterslide Slab on the Buachaille. There we let them blow in the wind. We built a cairn and came down again and hung about Jacksonville a little at a loss.

Although it happened so long ago I still get angry at the manner of Willie's death. Our innocent decision-making separated us that weekend. Matters of triviality kept some of us in the city. This was unusual for at that time we never missed a weekend away in the hills. So there was a chance to do something different, and as we discussed adventure fantasies in Glasgow's Danceland, Willie decided to join some others in a trip to friendly Ben A'n. For these reasons we were not with him when he fell unroped from Birch Wall and landed surprised and apologetic on the ledge before slipping over into the void below. Apologetic for what? Because he knew the route so well; had soloed it hundreds of times before, up and down, with all the hard variations, he seemed embarrassed to find himself on that ledge. It would have held him if he had been concentrating on his landing. That is what those who saw it said. I can never know and what does such regret matter now? We have no control over the fate that violates our futures. We can rage against our frustrations, our loss, the waste of his sweet life, but it happened. There is an end to it! And yet, the fact that I am writing this suggests that it has never ended.

I have a confession to make. Back in those early days when we were boys and bivouacked high in the Cobbler Corrie under the great stones to watch the stars and plan the next day's climbing, I thought Willie would be my eternal climbing partner. We would, I believed, work our way through the easy routes as required to build my unathletic frame into something resembling a climber. How foolish I was to think I could tie him to my mundane ambitions. Thus while I struggled with my horrendous inabilities he soared with better men. I remember how he eased up Whortleberry Wall as I lay Curved Ridge-bound, cursing my timidity and weakness. He then went on to greater things; a new line with Davie Todd on Slime Wall and the first ascent of Torro on Ben Nevis with John MacLean and Bill Smith.

Yet, we did manage **some good** climbs together. The one that keeps returning to my mind was that winter ascent of Agag's Groove on the Buachaille. Well, to be honest, it was not really a winter ascent. There was not much in the way of snow and ice on it. Just some patches on the second and last pitches whose easy angles allowed it to nestle there. It was probably just as well that winter had not clad the climb in severe winter dress for poorly equipped and naive as we were, it might have been too much. I remember the long axes and useless ex-army crampons we dangled on our belts.

I enjoyed that climb. Wrapped in double sweaters and anorak, balaclavas on our heads, we kept warm enough on the belays waiting to dash up each pitch as our turn came. We smiled at the people on Curved Ridge. They had followed our footsteps in the snow and ice up the Ridge only to become puzzled as to why they disappeared. It did not enter their minds that a party would have traversed down into Easy Gully to climb on the Rannoch Wall under these conditions. My youthful pride was swollen insufferably when they gasped in realisation of our position. But most of all I remember sitting on the large block-belay under the 'nose' as Willie tackled that most exposed section of the climb. How steady he was, his hands frozen, poised on that dark steepness above the void, his useless ice axe and crampons clanking at his side. The sky behind was a pure blue; the white clouds were stretched and curled into a vortex by the wind. I was hypnotised by it all. It was that feeling experienced when you sit on a ledge high on some precipice and raise your head to the sky. With only the steep rocks above for reference, you experience a strange detachment from the earth which captures your mind as does a vague feeling of vertigo.

We had already unroped when we came across the hardest part of the climb – the traverse along the top of the Rannoch Wall. There was a little groove filled with ice which gave us a moment of hesitation, conscious as we were of the empty wall beneath our feet. The last time I passed that way a year or so ago I noticed there was a piton hammered into the back of it.

Later, coming round the steep snow which girdled Crowberry Tower we met Davie Todd and Alex Fulton who had just completed an ascent of the Left Fork of Crowberry Gully. In a flurry of wind and snow we exchanged a few words before parting, they down Curved Ridge and us for the summit, before descending by way of Lagangarbh Coire.

The day was not yet over. On our descent of the Coire we came across two men sitting in the snow some way below the steep head-wall. They were members of a snow and ice course and one of them had just descended the Coire in an undignified, headlong fashion. Their instructor had gone down to Lagangarbh to bring up the stretcher. As we saw that these two were safe enough, we decided to go down to help the instructor with his heavy and awkward stretcher. This fellow lacked charm for on encountering us he merely grunted in reply to our offer of help, dropped the stretcher and set off up the hill leaving Willie and I to manhandle it to his stricken party.

We loaded the injured climber onto the stretcher and began to descend as the Coire filled with enthusiastic rescuers coming to help. It was in those days before official rescue teams had been invented, when rescues had to be carried out by whoever happened to be handy.

Down on the road at Altnafeadh someone was taking photographs as the stretcher was loaded into the waiting ambulance. As I watched the bearers, their features erased by the flashlights, Willie touched my arm and nodded his head in the direction of the dark winter road to Jacksonville. The job was done; quietly he had played his part. Together we stepped onto that road and walked away. It never entered my head that soon his friends would carry him from the hill.

Why do I think of these things after so long? I suppose I have always thought them somewhere in the recesses of my mind. They are fragments of memory half-consciously reflected upon as I have passed some place which has triggered them. So while for so many years nothing concrete emerged from my thoughts, I have always remembered. I have remembered every time I go up the Springburn Road; or at Ben A'n as I roped up to climb Birch Wall. I have remembered when I have sweated my way past the Waterslide Slab. It happened so long ago. I did not grieve then, but I grieve now. Middle age has released me from the ego of youth which denies mortality. It has released me from the belief that climbing is all and everything else nothing. Moreover, I must confess self interest here, for a couple of years ago on a most innocent expedition, I came as close to death as I would wish. The rotten snow of the head-wall of some obscure gully collapsed and sent me hurtling down its slope, my mind so occupied by the thought that the cornice must surely unzip and engulf me, I failed to notice that my ice-axe had poked a hole in my guts.

I realise that when we were young we did not talk of such things. It was all just fun, and to philosophise was unnecessary if not grounds for social rejection. But climbing wasted Willie, and only now do I ask the question; was it worth it? Can it be argued that climbing is such an important and rewarding activity, we must accept that some of our friends, if not ourselves, will die. That is the price we pay. Some would say the answer is no. Climbing, they argue, is in the last analysis, something which demands so much egoistical, physical and mental energy that it is inevitably a narrowing and constraining activity. It is a pointless pursuit and like religion a rage against the insignificance of man when confronted by the forces of nature.

Yet this is an academic argument and our lives were not governed thus. We came to climbing in our youth, not to understand it in relation to the meaning of life, but to seek and to find the romance of advanture. And it was not just the rock: it was the hills, the pubs, the weekends, the travel, and perhaps most of all, the people. Adventure, of course, is a relative concept. Something which can be adjusted to one's abilities and inclinations in any period of one's life. It has been the constant rediscovering of this which has kept me going into middle age, overcoming periods of inertia and disillusion-ment. Given my timidity and physical limitations, I was never going to get even near the standards of the friends of our youth. Yet I have travelled on many a mountain track, and along the way there have been a few minor triumphs. I grieve for Willie because he did not have the opportunity to do the same. From time to time we could have met to walk some mountain path, or climb some rock and recall the times gone by. Instead I am left to wonder at what might have been.

Married Man's Bothy Weekend

You know that the big groups and the old days have gone; know that when you manage to get out it is maybe as one of a pair, or even on your own. So and so has taken up kayaking or kung-fu; another is so unfit that the hill is out of the question. One is working overtime to pay for the new car; another has to visit the in-laws with the kids. And then every few years it happens. The excuses and impediments seem to disappear. A big group gets away with the chance to prove what Goethe says in *Faust*,

> It's not that age brings childhood back again,
> Age merely shows what children we remain.

It might have been the rumour of a new place where – amazingly – no one had ever been; Melgarve, high up by the dark fold of the Corrieyairack Pass. One or two tempted by near-by Munros undone; others by the fact that the place was driveable-to. Or by rumours of easy walks on the Wade military road. But the numbers increased, swelled, until a fleet of four cars assembled at the Dalwhinnie Transport café on a cold November night. The ground was showing the year's first touch of frost. The café was like something out of a Hopper painting; black without, bright and garish within. A morose group of locals looked as if they had waited a long time for the Greyhound Bus.

There was the Boomer and Mr. Ten Percent and the Dominie, with rumours of others possible, like Fishgut Mac. Altogether a round dozen if you included the dog Rusty, a golden retriever.

I had suggested the trip and I was worried. Firstly I had run out of petrol and free-wheeled down from the top of the Drumochter pass. The café's petrol pumps had long since, I noticed, been uprooted from the tarmac. After exchange of greeting someone suggested a rush in another of the fleet to Newtonmore where we caught a petrol station five minutes off closing. The can of petrol was added to the empty tank with the aid of a funnel made from a rolled-up café menu; the idea of the scientific brain of Mr. Ten Percent.

"This way we'll get about ninety percent of it in. Just pour and you'll be lucky to get half," he said sagely.

Then there was the next, unspoken worry. As I regarded my excited and expectant companions I recalled that I had never actually been to this bothy. But I had heard, on good evidence, that it was there and open and dossable. What if it wasn't? My popularity might decline, I felt. It seemed as if youth's big numbers were bringing back its unplanned unpredictability. But not its carefree thoughtlessness.

But it turned out to be there. After a drive from Laggan Bridge over the double-humped Wade's bridge at Garva, we ascended a steadily-deteriorating road. Grass grew on the crown of the causey and it poured with water. The moor was alive with deer; you simply drove between the huge cat's-eyes that lined the road. An owl flew at the car, raising its claws and flew off: hopefully the Owl of Minerva, bringing wisdom to those in quest. As the road worsened we slowed down and finally at walking-pace gained the black outline of the cottage.

"It's locked," said the first man out of the first car. My heart sank; my credibility was ruined! With an effort at coolness I suggested, "Try roon the back."

It was open. In fact, it wanted a front door, so open was it. It also needed repair. Windows were broken and lath missing. Downstairs was used partly as a byre; a strong smell of cow piss pervaded the place. But upstairs was fine. The doors did not fit but they were there and so was the floor. What more could a man ask of a doss? I was so relieved I vowed to come back and do some work on it in the summer, as an offering of thanks.

It was dry and starry when we arrived and light powder-snow had made a promise of the black hills for the morrow. The party had left the café before closing time and no one drank, thinking of the next day's plans. No Saturday hangovers in mid-life. Tea, a chat, and bed.

The evening's promise was foresworn the next day. During the night the heavens had opened; the road was a torrent. Cloud lay low on hills russet with dead bracken. Plans to eliminate rounded mental obsessions, like Geal Charn and Carn Liath were abandoned, even when it lifted a little. The speed of the moving cloud and spindrift on the hills showed it would be a nasty day.

But there was a wonderful historical middle-aged alternative out the front door. The old military road, built in the 1730s to pacify the Jacobite Highlands, led up and into the pass. That would do for an off-day and maybe the day after would set fair.

The old military road has lasted its 250 years well. Much of the foundation of broken stone is intact, as are the drainage runnels. Many of the old bridges are collapsed but the one out behind Melgarve has been handsomely repaired. The party walked at a leisurely pace, observing the grey lightshafts penetrating the cloud and the moving tones of colour on the moor. The road would last their lifetime out. They were reversing the route of the Jacobite Army in 1745, Erchie looking like the ghost of a lost straggler.

Just below Corrieyairack Hill the road suddenly zig-zags up sharply to the summit of the pass. Here were still remains of the restraining embankments to prevent erosion. The main threat to this monument of civil engineering would not appear to be the weather but those motor-cyclists and four-wheeled vehicles whose tracks we observed, tearing up the surface of the road. Then the rain washes deep channels in it and carries it away.

At the top sleet started and the cloud came down. Some decided to call it a day and descended by the zig-zags to collect firewood for the evening. Another group wanted to cross back by Corrieyairack Hill to the bothy and continued. They were rewarded, for the late afternoon turned into a roseate glow and the cloud lifted high as the wind dropped. Stoves were already roaring, aperitifs were being taken, the fire was set when that party returned. Without a four-footed beastie that had been part of it and without its owner.

Questions flew. Erchie replied, "We were up the tap o' the Corrieyairack Hill, when Rusty shot aff, chasin a group o' stags. They were playin wi him, lettin him catch up and then speedin aff.

Young Paul hared aff aifter him and was last seen ploughin through the snaw taewards the Findhorn."

We all had a good laugh since we assumed that once tired of its chase the dog would return to its pursuing master. More went for wood, others ate and drank. All were pleased, fine pleased, with the bothy, the character of the glen, the historicity of the surroundings. Night fell, time passed. A semi-silence followed; Paul had not come back.

Then we heard his footsteps coming up the stairs, turned round as he entered the door. Before we could ask, he did; "Is the dog back?" But hardly were the words uttered when our eyes gave him the negative answer.

He had contoured the top. Looking, seeing nothing. The dog must have headed north into the trackless country towards the Findhorn river. He was young, untrained. He would not find his way back. A heavy frost was gathering, there were flakes of snow. They fell as silently as everyone's unspoken thoughts. The beast had had it. As a gesture to Paul, parties wandered up and down the road shouting and flashing lights. But it was clearly hopeless, despite Ten Percent's calculations – cartographic, logarithmic and meteorological. He was convinced he could work out the exact map reference at which the dog would emerge. I told him he could wait there; I was going back to the bothy.

No man is an island. But no man can ever feel the exact register of another's sorrow. As Paul slumped miserably in a corner, others offered hope, condolences. But gradually the effect of the fire (supplemented by carting in coal) and the drink had its effect. People relaxed, unwound. Shirts were unbuttoned, belts loosened. A few tales were swopped and then, when Erchie started off with 'It's dark as a dungeon, down in the mine,' we were away. Half-forgotten songs were remembered, choruses were joined in and people who had not sung for years, even sang solo to an appreciative audience, ear drums dulled by whisky, wine and beer. One of the company got out a flute, gave us a few jigs and reels and accompanied the singers. Another expounded to his listener on the etymology of Gaelic place names amidst the din. His hand reached automatically for a dod of chalk and his eyes for a blackboard, as the Dominie in him overcame the disappointed Munroist.

I had known him years ago; in Aberdeen, when the times they were a-changin. We had had our differences then over the interpretation of Marx's 'Capital' and the class nature of the Soviet Union. And over a woman. The latter dispute had led to O.K. Corral stuff in the Cove Bay Hotel. And later to an embarrassed apology by myself. Then I did not know where he was on the face of the earth for near 20 years. Till one day we were standing side by side on the terraces at Love Street; both fathers, teachers, Dons supporters and Munro-baggers. A wild Trotskyist no more but a pillar of the Labour Party, world expert on the history of Coatbridge and his local golf club's historian. A candidate to become, in the fullness of time, a freeman of the burgh.

He appeared to exercise a restraining influence on the wilder excesses of the Boomer. The first time we three went away Erchie took no drink and was a perfect gentleman. This was at Kinbreak, where the Dominie, eyes glazed, spent twelve hours doing the ridge from Sgur Mor to Sgurr na Ciche. Exhausted on return he lay prostrate, gasping and expounding on the likely derivations of all the peaks he had crossed, with the passionate intensity formerly reserved for a recitation of Stalin's crimes.

"Bidean isn't peak," he cried, "it's Spidean, spike." And fell back, exhausted, delirious.

Life, The Universe and everything was passed in review. One lad gave a rendering of the 'Bonnie Lass o' Fyvie'. At the end of every verse after the tenth the company clapped in relief and hope. "No, no, there's more!", he cried earnestly. He felt he'd never sung better,

> There's mony a bonny lass in the Howe o' Auchterless
> There's mony a bonny lass in the Garioch-o
> There's mony a bonny quaen in the toun o' Aiberdeen
> But the floo'er o' them a' bides in Fyvie-o.

At first the good-humour was a bit forced, in order to blot out Paul's sorrow. But as the fire bleezed (Erchie forbad anyone bed till he'd

Erchie Boomer

blown a big hole in the ozone layer by consuming all the fuel and bigger holes in our brain cells by consuming all the drink), so spirits were thoroughly warmed. But on turning, there was always the Figure in the corner. In some ways it was a relief to douse the fire and the candles, for then it was invisible.

With the social graces of a charging elephant in a mine-field, Erchie means no harm; but his humour can have a cutting edge to it, whiles. We heard him going out in the middle of the night, doubtless to remove from his body some of the gallons of liquid he had imbibed. My heart sank when I heard him cry out, "Hey, Paul, that daft dug o' yours is doon here!"

I waited for the explosion of grief and anger this would bring. Instead I found myself showered with water, wet paws in my face, hot tongue lolling out. It was back! It had been out in a howling dark wilderness for 14 hours and had found its way back in a snowstorm. What a tale it could tell if it were given speech! It would out-do White Fang itself. Paul was so delighted he jumped in his car and drove ten dark miles alone in the middle of the night to tell his life-partner that all was well.

"It's weel kent he's nae bairns yet," quipped one cynic.

"I bet he was less feart o' Route Major, than he was o' seein the wife withoot the dog," added another. "Alpine routes are naethin tae a woman's fury."

In the morning all was relief and jollity, the doggy tale told over and over again. The party split up but promises were made to meet again soon. The worried organiser of this trip was unanimously elected unofficial meets secretary with a remit for the early New Year. It was a glorious winter's day; sky blue, hills white, dazzling. Some went off to tackle a dreary Corbett near the bothy, at Erchie's instigation. "Corbetts," muttered one in mock disgust, "He used tae be a Hard Severe man."

I myself had a footnote to the trip to complete. I had arranged to meet Fishgut Mac for a day out in Glen Banchor. He had not been able to make the bothy (a pity, since he would have raised the musical tone) but a day out had been found to be possible.

We climbed A' Chailleach and Carn Sgulain, lunching in the ruined stalkers' bothy on the slopes. Fireplace gone, but table still there, it gave us a brief respite against the cold. On top the wind rose and we hurried to the second peak, where mist came down, and navigated off the plateau. Here we found a hideous spongy track, drainage totally destroyed, made by Argocats across the moor.

"Ye missed a guid nicht," I told Mac. "Since ye wernae there, I'd tae dae the singin."

His pow wrinkled in disbelief.

Mac was sad he had missed the night; he had not done an overnight in a bothy in 10 years. He was also sad because Ewan

MacColl had just died and he had done a radio broadcast on him from his folk record collection. But the hill worked its magic and we parted with promises. His was,

"I'll try and get sometime, if ye promise tae leave the singin tae me."

Back in the car with Alec for a fish supper and Guinness in Dunkeld. He was a novitiate to bothy life but showed promise of being a late convert. He had proved wonderfully useful too in getting out of the car in the pouring rain to open the gates across the Wade's road. And he had great skills. Knew instantly, when the car kept cutting out, that the coil was drenched by the puddles and got out to remedy it with a rag while I held the wheel, apologising for my mechanical ignorance. I felt really embarrassed, just like the time in Kintail when the two Doctors practically fought each other to change my wheel when I had a puncture.

"Weel, ye had it a' there on yer first trip. Romance, history, adventure, archaeology..."

"Archaeology?"

"Aye, Erchie Boomer, he's a bit prehistoric. Maybe that's far the Erchie comes fae. And a' for the very modest sum that I'll be lifting aff ye for food, petrol and guidance at Dunkeld."

"Minus the charge for the car repair."

He was a quick learner.

The dog had come back. But not the sweet bird of youth, it never would. Goethe was right. We lose youth, but remain children. But he also said, in the second part of *Faust*,

Whoever always strives,
That man we can save.

Children, but saved? The road was disintegrating, grass-grown. But it would last our lifetime and we had got along it to our refuge.

Doubtless the reader assumes I never got back to repair Melgarve. But that is the trouble with middle-age, we tend to keep our promises, unlike in youth when we forget them. So the next Spring I spent a weekend there dividing my time between wandering over obscure Monadh Liath Munros and fixing the door, the windows, the floor of the bothy. On return a month later with a plane, brush, shovel and so forth, I met a local from down Laggan way who gave me an invitation I could not refuse, to a piece of midsummer madness.

I came with my son, a friend and his sons on midsummer eve. We found the place possessed by some unpleasant Edinburgh public schoolboys who had come in Daddy's Volvo. (Daddy, they told us, knew the gamekeeper). They gave us to understand that they thought we were trespassing and left next day after collectively and pointedly using the bothy as a toilet.

But oh what a contrast the lads of Laggan were! They arrived in droves – real people; butchers, carpenters and the like, invited themselves to share our fire and shared with us their drink. Fine whisky and deep, ruby, home-made wine. Some were members of the defeated Newtonmore shinty Cammanachd Cup Final team, which called for a dram of condolence. They offered to 'sort out' the public schoolboys for us but our mature moderation restrained their youthful desire to execute summary justice.

"That's the only wye tae deal wi these folk," was the opinion of the shinty-playing butcher.

They were up to hold back the night. To drive to the top of the Pass and light a fire at the summer solstice. To try, unavailingly, to ward off the encroaching shades of winter. They had repaired the road to enable them to drive along it. On their return they feasted and drank at the bothy; an old oil-drum, halved, serving as a barbecue. We celebrated this prehistoric tradition with them well into the night but had to decline (the burden of paternity) the invitation to the dance at Laggan. We returned to our sleeping children, the bad taste of the other occupants wiped from our mouths by the good wine of Laggan.

Hold back the night! We build our solstice fire on the mountains, against the shortening of the days, every time we set foot on them. A fine, but unavailing fire.

A Doggerel Ballad.

(Tune: Somewhere between 'My Heart's in the Hielands' and 'The Old Orange Flute').

Chorus:

My dug's in the Hielands, my dug is nae here
My dug's in the Hielands a-chasing the deer
A-chasing the wild deer, aff through the snaw
Whar is my doggie? Gey far awa!

Twas up by Melgarve whar the cauld north winds blaw
Young Paul took his doggie a walk in the snaw
On top o' Corrieyairack they met wi some stags
And Rusty set aff in pursuit through peat hags.

Young Paul he took aff in a terrible fricht
But the big happy doggie was seen lost frae sicht
Heading for Findhorn it noo was quite clear
Rusty wouldnae gie up his pursuit o' the deer.

Noo young Paul cam back in the dark, wi nae dog
His head bowed in grief, he sat doon on a log
Then aff tae a phone box, tae be telt o' course
'Find that poor doggie, or for you it's divorce!'

The answer o' course, it was held by wan seer
Wha had a sure hunch whar the dug would appear,
Was ninety percent sure he'd find the lost pup
But like a' o' his facts, this ane was made up.

Though ithers there were wi mair personal woes,
Like the Dominie Pete wha'd bagged nae Munroes
They a' offered Paul their deep sympathy
In the form o' a dram; he would only tak tea.

The auld sangs were sung, the tin whistle did blaw
Coal whoomed up the lum, and the sticks did an a'
And bottles o' whisky and gallons o' beer
Pit the rest o' the crew in a verra guid cheer.

Paul sat in a corner, a terrible sicht
Spoke tae naebody the hale o' the nicht
His nerves they were fankled, his mind in a fog
For naething could mak him forget his big dog.

Noo Erchie went oot in the deid o' the nicht
Staggered drunken doonstairs withoot ony licht
Tripped ower a wet heap and fell on his back
Boomed out tae young Paul, "Yer doggie's cam back!"

Come a' ye dog owners tak a warning by me
Make siccar yer doggie is nae like Rusty
Whan you see fine deer stags set aff at great speed
Tak care that yer daft mutt is safe on the lead.

(With apologies to Walter Scott, William MacGonegal, Fishgut
Mac, and Erchie who thought up the chorus lines.)

A View From the Ridge

When climbers attempt to climb a mountain they often choose to do so by ascending a ridge. Such a method of ascent has much to recommend it, for not only does it allow a convenient method of access to the mountain, sometimes hard, sometimes easy, it also affords splendid views of other parts of the mountain. In this way the climber can learn more about the mountain so that on his return he can explore further its other aspects.

What you have read represents our view from the ridge. It is a personal view shaped by our experiences. It could not have been otherwise. And what we have found in these experiences did not always match what we had been led to expect by our reading of the literature of Scottish mountaineering.

To obtain the view we started with a journey. As boys we played the games of adventure. These could be rather nasty affairs – genocide in short trousers and dirty knees. Or, less bloodthirsty, scoring the winning goal in the cup final at Hampden. Yet as we grew, we felt by some mysterious process the pull of places, unknown and unseen, beyond the streets in which we fought and played. Our bikes provided the link between the adventure of boyhood and that of adolescence. We had probed the city limits in sweaty expeditions, and wanted to push beyond the line of hills glimpsed far off. Thus while the generation before had walked into the hills, we, the children of the new affluence, one day cycled off to see the mountains which would excite our future ambitions. That first journey signalled the end of childhood and the end of illusionary adventure. The hills were real as was the adventure they promised. We were intrigued by their shapes and summits and wondered about breaking from the chains of the metalled road to explore the mysteries above. The first journey was the first of many; journeys from boyhood into adolescence and beyond into adulthood.

A journey into the hills that was to determine the shape of our future lives.

We were very lucky coming to the hills when we did. We caught the end of an era. The great proleterian revolution had passed its height but its values and its characters lingered on. We were much influenced by them both.

The hills were uncrowded – it was possible to spend a weekend in Bob Scott's and have it to yourself. Ben Nevis, winter or summer was curiously quiet. There were no queues on Agag's Groove whose holds were wonderfully unpolished.

The lack of crowds meant there was no market for the fancy gear we have today. Equipment was basic; people still improvised, making their own gaiters or cutting down old macintoshes to make anoraks. We also spent a great deal of effort trying not to look like climbers; ex-army tartan trews or jeans, American army combat-jackets and eight piece bunnets made up our group's particular disguise.

Actual climbing equipment, although an advance on that of previous generations, was also barely adequate. We had hawser laid nylon ropes, one or two slings and steel karabiners. There were no nuts and few pitons to ensure safety. We used to jam the Fisherman's Knots in our slings into cracks in the fond belief they would hold a fall. The belay after the traverse on Punster's Crack on the Cobbler was one place such a tactic was utilised. Luckily this theory was never, in my experience, put to the test. Rock boots were almost unknown and could only be obtained by sending to France for them. If someone owned a pair you knew he was a 'hard' man, for opinion dictated that climbs up to severe and often beyond, must be climbed in big boots. To break this rule was unthinkable. Our first pairs were large and bendy. Some did not even have boots and I was taken up my first climb in Glencoe, Agag's Groove, by a man wearing shoes shod in commando soles. There were those who were not impressed by new-fangled devices such as rubber soles, for in the deep and secret corries of the Cairngorms, and even in the gentle Trossachs, we saw the last of the men whose boots were dressed in tricouni nails. They sparked their way up climbs pronouncing on the superior technique they forced upon their user. Rubber soles, they forecast lugubriously, were sure to breed a generation of sloppy incompetent climbers who sacrificed good technique on the easy altar of technology.

Transport was also fairly basic. Hitch-hiking and the club bus were our principal modes of travel, methods which added extra dimensions to the adventure and camaraderie of the weekend. The buses had a physical complexion which mirrored our society of vagabonds. At the front were the courting couples, usually very quiet and not long for the scene – nest-building would see to that! In the middle and more noisy were the card players – pontoon was their sport, and the winner one weekend could be assured that the losers would follow him to his choice of location the next. A good player could shape the development of Scottish climbing by attracting large numbers of leading climbers to particular areas. At the rear were the singers – their proud boast, Glasgow to Fort William without repeating a song. Sometimes the songs could get a bit rough and this inevitably led to trouble when some became offended. Our crowd were barred from the Glasgow University Club bus for such behaviour.

While the club bus cost money, barring the odd crunching brush with a snowdrift, it at least got you to your destination. This was not always the case with hitch-hiking. The school shed at Tarbet, or the phone box at Tyndrum – before the railway bothy was discovered – often gave shelter to the traveller who had given up hope in the early hours of Saturday morning. Hitch-hiking home on a winter's Sunday night could also be an unrewarding activity as vehicles passed at a rate of about one every half an hour. There was nothing worse than standing frozen outside Cameron's barn at Altnafeadh in Glencoe watching the lights of an approaching car illuminate the dark sky, even though it may still have been several miles away. As you watched the lights reflecting off the clouds twist and turn like a searchlight probing for enemy aircraft, anticipation built – would this be the one to end your icy agony? Hopes were usually dashed as the car sped by unheeding, its rear lights to remain in sight for some time seen floating in the blackness which hid the Rannoch Moor.

Despite the uncertainty of these travel arrangements we went away every weekend, winter and summer. We never trained in gyms, relying on constant activity at weekends to keep us fit. Yet, paradoxically, we wasted time as if there were no tomorrows. All-night card games, monumental hangovers and a vicious ball game called 'wee heidies' kept us away from the hill, sometimes when we did not have bad weather as an excuse. Time and opportunities when you are young seem to be in endless supply.

The whole experience had a magical effect on everyone we knew, for few did not feel a subtle change take place within them. Our minds, once shackled by chains forged by school and work, began to rebel against the narrow boundaries of our alloted positions as we search for something better than the factory or the office. For many the answer came in world travel. The Alps, Antarctica, North and South America, the Himalayas, Australia and New Zealand, felt the tread of ourselves and our contemporaries' feet as we sought future shape to our spirits. Some liked what they saw in these places and stayed. Others remained true to their roots and returned home from their travels intent on satisfying a curiosity which could only be slaked in places of Higher Education.

Yet this is only one side of our story, for the values of the proletarian mountaineer had their negative side as well as their positive. Forget the admiration Murray had for his stout companions. The climbing world into which we were initiated was governed by sets of values which would not have been alien to rutting stags. However the prizes in this male hierarchy were not the human equivalent of hinds, but the prestige of first ascents and hard climbs. As a consequence one found among groups of climbers who were meant to be friends, rather than rivals, a metaphorical clashing of antlers which brought forth the wounds of envy, greed and the disparagement of the efforts of others. I remember arriving at a well-known centre for mountaineering instruction to be warned by a friend, a leading figure of his generation, not to climb with Big Rab from the village as he was very unsafe. Only later did it emerge that Big Rab's sin was not his lack of care, but that he had climbed a new line which my friend had discovered and was working on. Forgetting that he too had acted in this way in the past, my friend's revenge was the attempted isolation of Big Rab.

It is our realisation of common human frailty which gives a clue to something about this book which may have disconcerted the reader, succoured as he or she may have been on the more traditional type of outdoor-adventure literature. Since the beginning of mountain-eering, climbers have written about their endeavours. At first this comprised of simple descriptions of what was achieved. If any excuse was needed for the bizarre enjoyment of climbing hills, scientific discovery provided it. However, by the end of the Edwardian age such simplicity faded along with the generation which had spawned it. In its place came climbers who returned from their struggles on the steeps, and their cold bivouacs with tales forged in the language of the gods. Climbing had to be something bigger than the slash of adze upon the ice, or the scrape of hobnail upon rock. It was no longer sufficient to describe the act of climbing. Climbing had become the proving ground of character or a vehicle in the search for ultimate truths. Our view would deny this.

Take the notion that climbing builds character. We have no reason to doubt that the companions of Murray were anything less than he described. Stout fellows were they. Gentle yet strong, quiet yet courageous, and uniformily cheerful even under the most appalling conditions. Rather than whinge and moan, these philoso-pher kings would smoke a contemplative pipe all the while ruminating on the human condition. We came to the hills seeking the company of such gods, and while we found many who were quite normal, there were people like Joe.

If Joe appears to have been under-written in his brief appearances in this work, it is because of the feeling that the world is not yet ready for his scatological sense of humour and other forms of bizarre behaviour. His personality, moreover, suffered from some deeply ingrained contradictions. On the one hand he was a street fighting man, ready to do battle at the least excuse. On the other, he was terrified of the dark. In those far-off days when we used to camp out under the boulders of the Cobbler Corrie, Joe used to make sure he was never there first in case he had to endure the dark night on his own. Thus he would sit in the bar of what was the old Ross Hotel in Arrochar, drinking a few pints until he saw the torch lights of his companions ascend the hill across the loch. Only then would he make his way to the howff. Once he miscalculated and was found under the Narnain Boulder with every candle he possessed alight. When his approaching companions did not answer to calls he sank to his knees calling on his God for salvation.

There were others who, to a lesser degree, were like him. One summer when working on the ski-lift in Glen Coe, I shared Jacksonville with a young man famous for his lack of attention to his personal freshness. People used to say he returned from seasons in the Alps wearing the same underpants he wore when he had left Glasgow some months earlier; white when he went out they were green on his return. Thus, one evening, when he declared his intention to wash his feet in the river before going down to the pub, my curiosity was aroused enough to follow him out of the hut to watch. He duly plunged into the burn still wearing his light fell-boots. These he soaped assiduously before wading to the far bank and squelching off down the road to the Kingshouse, there to drink his beer while his boots oozed puddles on the floor.

Another was Black Rab who had so comprehensively silenced the police at the 'burning of the boat (see *Mountain Days and Bothy Nights*) at Glen Brittle. Dressed most incongruously as an Indian chief, he chased a companion from the bar of the Glencoe Hotel, commandeered a car from a bemused tourist and drove it through a large marquee at some Highland event at Ballachullish before escaping from the avenging law by disappearing into the hills beyond. Rab, as he used to describe himself, certainly was the 'biggest no-care cunt' in Glen Coe.

Characters they certainly were, but they could never be offered as role models on Outward Bound courses. Yet while they were not what we expected they held us in the grip of a horrible fascination. After my relatively sheltered upbringing, Joe was a particular revelation: the ultimate free spirit to whom the conventions, so rigorously adhered to in my earlier life, meant nothing. He was a dangerous man to know, and I was both attracted and repelled.

It goes without saying that such men were not drawn to climbing in order to discover ultimate truths to be found behind the beauty of the mountains. Even if they had read Murray, it was not likely that they would have discussed such philosophies while playing darts in the public bar of the Kingshouse. To have done so would have invited a great deal of unhealthy suspicion.

The people we knew belonged firmly to the oral tradition of Scottish mountaineering, and for this reason their lives, their motivations, their activities and their views are not widely represented in the mountaineering literature of Scotland. Despite the fact that some of them were among the leading exponents of both rock and ice climbing of their generations, they were neither writers of articles, nor were they much written about. Few climbers write about the opposition. (Marshall's article *The Initiation* SMCJ XXXIII 1984 is a welcome exception to this rule).

Climbers may be expected by their readers to return from their walls and their ledges with high falutin' visions of truth and beauty to explain, perhaps, why they climb and how changes to their character or mental states have been wrought deep inside them. The oral tradition knows no such constraints. Consequently what we knew was a kind of reality. Our companions climbed because their egos demanded it of them. Their place in the pecking order relied on it. Thus, for them there were neither Holy Grails nor Golden Fleece to be sought. There was no Arcadia to discover.

Other realities crowded in, for in our experience you cannot leave entirely the tensions, strife and contradictions of wider society behind. Climbing may give relief – the satisfaction of completing some achievable goal in wild and difficult places – but the problems are still there on your return.

The land with which we struggled so hard was neutral in all this. It was wet and mean. Our muscles ached on the night marches into bothies. We hated the land – the stony path which climbed and plunged and climbed again without reason in the dark wet night, the rain running down our necks and mixing uncomfortably with the sweat of our bodies. We loved the land, and marched under a moon which, with the help of the snow-covered ground, turned night into day; or woke early to watch the sun rise through the mist over the moor. The climbers had their reasons to be there. The land was just the land. No more and no less.

So when we travelled, be it in search of the energy of America or the land of eternal youth in the Outer Hebrides, we, in the end, kept that reality. In America, while we saw the beauty of its mountains, immersed ourselves in 'On the Road' fantasies and enjoyed the generosity of our friends, we also felt an ugly narrowness – a life-threatening force which leaked from the small towns and fuelled the bombers above Merced. In the Hebrides we enjoyed the windswept wilds, but saw the slow death of the culture and knew the old men must die. For these reasons we resisted settling in the Highlands or emigrating to America.

Did this make us any less worthy than the poets, the character-builders or those who sought the ultimate truths? We must deny this. We were worthy simply by being there. We lit the fire, and made room for strangers at the ingle-nook. We told the tales and sang the songs. We passed on the feelings that what we did was right. Good and bad, we were what we were and could not have been anything else.

In the fire we found something else which was important. A continuity. In the fire which consumes we have seen the deaths of those we knew. Bobby Gow in Crowberry Gully, Big Willie Gordon on Ben A'n. Eddie Cairns while abseiling on the East face of North Buttress on the Buachaille, Alistair Foster of altitude sickness in Africa, John Cunningham in the wild seas of Wales. We still remember them. They return from time to time, called forth by places, tales of deeds done, a rummage through old photographs.

In the ashes of the fire we have seen rebirth. Our enthusiasm for the hills has ebbed and flowed, and now in middle-age we play different games from those of our youth. Thus while we may spend a week in the hut at Scavaig, or still sleep out in the heather some summer's night, we do not go away every weekend. Instead we gently collect Munros on a Sunday, or spend our summers seeking out some untaxing rock climb missed in that blurred time of youth. Work and family make demands on our time. Yet the hills have remained constant, bringing us back again and again to the fundamental realities we find there. Every trip, no matter the weather, brings something. The winter ridge glimpsed through clearing mist, the sky lit by marching bars of light, the snow bunting on the summit of Ben Nevis, the story in the pub or song by the bothy fire. Experiences such as these are always possible and explain why we do not give in.

And now our children come behind us. We cannot assume that they will want to follow, to imitate or advance what we have done. But we can tell and let them choose. What we offer, we hope, is something of value. Our view from the ridge. The hills, the people, the fun and the tragedy. What it was really like in a time which has almost passed.